CAREER CONVICT

A NOVEL

HEIKE PHELAN

Career Convict

by Heike Phelan

© Copyright 2020 Heike Phelan

ISBN 978-1-9163490-0-1

Published by Black Horse Publishing

Web Address https://www.facebook.com/heikephelanbooks/

E-Mail: blackhorsepublishing@yahoo.com

DEDICATION

For my darling husband, the inspiration for this book, without whose support and encouragement this second book in the Convict series would never have been written.

ACKNOWLEDGEMENTS

Huge thanks to my amazing editor Paul Smith at Wise Grey Owl (www.wisegrayowl.com). His 'brutal' editing wasn't as bad as I anticipated, but his advice and suggestions have been invaluable.

As always my undying devotion and gratitude to Matthew Schiffert for his unending support and guidance during the process of writing this book, and life.

Huge thanks to Mary Jayne Baker for stepping in at the last minute to create the book cover. I probably drove her mad.

1

He had been driving the young son of his fellow outlaw friend Lenny home when Youngster had received a text message from his girlfriend saying she was being harassed by a guy in Starbucks. They headed off to rescue the girl. William pulled into the car park of the restaurant next door to the Starbucks in question. Youngster jumped out of the car and headed over to the door. He went inside to find his girlfriend seated at the corner table arguing with a tall well built white man. Even seated he looked big, towering over Youngster's petite girlfriend. He was pointing aggressively at her and hissing through his teeth that he could be a far better boyfriend to her than the loser kid she's with. Melody had attempted to leave but had been hemmed in by her choice of table.

"Come on Melody, we're leaving," Youngster said as he took hold of her hand and pulled her out of the corner placing himself as a barrier between her and the rancorous guy.

"What the fuck. We're having a conversation so fuck off and mind your own business," Mr Aggressive said as he pushed Youngster across the table. Youngster lost his balance and broke his fall on the little round table.

He saw Melody run for the door whilst he was sprawled across the table. He knocked the remains of a coffee over, which splattered across his t-shirt. This infuriated him. He was particular about how he looked. He had a rigid grooming regime and liked to look sharp unconditionally. As he made to stand upright again and face Mr Aggressive, he slid his hand into his waistband.

"Why are you bothering my girlfriend?" Youngster asked.

The last word had barely left his mouth when he received a thunderous blow to the side of his head. Youngster staggered back against the wall. He was seeing stars in front of his eyes and managed to stop himself from falling over, but had to lean against the wall to give his eyes a chance to refocus.

"She won't be your girlfriend for long," sneered Mr Aggressive, taunting as Youngster tried to collect himself, "She's too good for you."

Still with his hand underneath his t-shirt, Youngster fiddled around then slowly exposed what he had hidden. In his hand was a Bowie hunting knife with an eight inch blade. Mr Aggressive looked down at Youngster's hand but barely had time to register it before Youngster stepped forward into the big man and plunged the knife into his stomach. He withdrew slightly and pushed it back in trying to push it even further through into body. Mr Aggressive looked at him with shock in his eyes as he slumped over towards Youngster. Being a good foot shorter and a hundred and fifty pounds lighter than Mr Aggressive, Youngster couldn't hold the guy's weight for long. His reverie ended when he heard someone scream. He pulled the blade out and pushed Mr Aggressive away from him as he sidestepped towards the door. He looked to where Mr Aggressive lay moaning across the table, whilst blood poured from his stomach. When the blood reached the edge of the table, it poured in a viscous stream onto the floor forming a pool by his feet.

Youngster heard voices shouting to call for the police. He scanned around the cafe and saw shocked faces staring at him, albeit from a position at the back of the cafe well away from the potential firing line. Youngster opened the door and ran out. As he sprinted across the car park to where William was parked, waiting for him, he looked around for Melody. She had gone. He jumped in the car, slammed the door shut and shouted at William to drive. William took one look at Youngster covered in coffee stains and blood and took off, wheels screeching.

William drove towards one of his rental houses from where he was currently selling drugs.

"What the fuck happened in there," William asked. "I saw Melody come running out and disappear down the street, and now here you are covered in blood. What the fuck,"

Youngster looked at William with as innocent face as he could muster.

"It just happened. He punched me and I stabbed him."

"Are you fucking crazy?" William said. "Where the fuck did you get the knife?"

"It was in your glove-box. It's the one you bought at the gun show last week." Youngster confessed.

"Oh my fucking God! Where's the knife now?"

Youngster took it out of his pocket and handed it to William. The blood on it was smeared over the blade and starting to dry.

"Get your togs off and get in the shower. There are clothes in the wardrobe. I'm going out to get rid of these. Stay here and do not open the door to anyone." With that William left.

2

William was gone for several hours.

He was not happy about losing his knife. He had spent months researching and looking for that knife. As a collector of vintage and historical weapons, he spent a lot of time visiting shows and events which catered to his interest in weaponry. He wasn't as particular with firearms, always making sure to have the newest and most modern weapons he could find on the street. Either from purchasing or stealing, it didn't matter to William. He did have a sizeable collection of historical firearms from muskets to shotguns but knives were a different matter. William loved the history of knives, daggers, swords and other blades that had been used in conflicts throughout history. He also loved knives as a silent weapon, his weapon of choice when he was out tip-toeing at night, breaking into houses. His favourite houses were the ones with large doggy doors he could climb through, or those with an attached garage, as most people tended to leave the door from the garage to the house unlocked.

William also wanted to hide the car. A bright red Mustang was noticeable. He drove it into the two car garage of another house he owned. He took the bloody clothes out through the house into the large garden and started a fire in an old oil drum he kept in the garden for just such purposes. He fed the bloody shirt and trousers slowly onto the fire and watched them burn. He kept the fire flaring until the clothes were nothing but ashes. He went back inside the three bedroom, two bathroom home which was in an upper-class suburban area. Absolutely no one knew he had this property, and that's how he intended it to stay.

William picked up the phone and called for a pizza. He then went to the fridge and pulled out a beer. In the living room, he slumped down on the couch and placed his feet on the coffee table. This house was a refuge from his own crazy life. He had taken great pleasure finding unique period furniture for it and the oak coffee table was well up to William's feet crashing down on it.

He was feeling angry with Youngster. William had known the boy for his whole life as Youngster's father Lenny and himself had grown up together in children's homes, foster care and living on the streets, committing crimes together for survival. He gave Lenny a call to let him know what happened whilst he waited for his pizza to turn up.

"The stupid little fucker," raged Lenny. "He's been doing so much stupid shit since he's been seeing that girl Melody. There's no talking to the little bastard any-more, he thinks he knows it all."

"What do you want me to do with him?" William asked. "I've left him in one of my rent houses for now, told him to stay there whilst I get rid of shit."

"Let the little fucker stay there a while and stew, see how things play out." Lenny advised.

After William put the phone down, he jumped up and went into the kitchen to wash the Bowie knife. He looked at it admiringly. It had a bone handle rounded at the end on the edge side, an eight inch blade sharpened on both sides and the distinct sterling silver guard at the hilt for which Bowie knives are famous. Although it wasn't an original, it was one of the Bowie knives made and exported to the US from Sheffield, England from the 1850's onward. William hadn't even had the chance to have it professionally valued.

He turned the taps on in the sink until the water warmed then laid the knife and it's decorated leather sheath in the water. After giving it chance to soak and loosen the dried blood, William used a soft cloth to gently scrub at the joins and angles to make sure the blood was washed away. When he was satisfied it was thoroughly cleaned, he towelled it dry then placed it on the work top. Once again he was contemplating the rash stupidity of the boy when he heard a knock at the front door. After peering through the peep-hole, he opened the door to the pizza delivery guy. William looked him up and down, surprised to see his dishevelled appearance and jacket torn down the sleeve.

"What happened to you?" He asked in greeting.

"A couple of punks on the street tried to pick a fight with me at my last drop off. I managed to run back to my car before they did more than grab at me." As he said this he looked forlornly at the sleeve hanging off his jacket, still shaken from the encounter. He handed the pizza over to William.

"Hang on whilst I get you some cash," William said in reply.

William strolled into the kitchen and fished around in his jean's pocket for some money and came out with a fifty dollar note. He didn't have anything smaller. He also picked up the knife, replaced it in the still damp sheath and went back to the front door.

"Here you go," William said as he handed over the fifty. "Keep the change."

Pizza man looked at the fifty dollar note in his hand and smiled. 'Thanks man, appreciate it.'

"Here take this, you'll have something to protect yourself next time someone tries to pick a fight." William slid the knife inside the guy's pizza delivery bag then shut the door and returned to the couch to eat.

That took care of the knife. He was sorry to lose it, but there was no alternative but to be rid of it.

Youngster took a long hot shower then dressed in clothes he found in the wardrobe. He then plopped down on the couch in the sitting room. That was when the shock of what he had done set in. He broke out in a sweat, as much from the hot shower as the thoughts of his actions. He started shaking and was unable to hold his hands steady.

What have I done? Well that guy shouldn't have been hitting on my girlfriend. It's his own fault. He got what he deserved.

Youngster tried to convince himself of truth of his assertion until it no longer sounded rational. Much as he tried the reality was that hitting on someone's girlfriend was not justification for killing him, ending his life and in such a brutal way. He started to cry at first tears rolling down his cheeks, then sobbing., followed by dramatic self pitying wailing and shouting. He stood, shouted and cursed whilst aggressively kicking any piece of furniture that was in his way. Unfortunately the furniture wasn't up to that kind of treatment. After he ran out of steam he retreated to an equally self pitying whimper.

He tried to pull himself together and thought about his actions. He had taken the Bowie knife from William's glove box earlier in the day when he had driven the Mustang out to buy smokes. He had been looking for loose change in the glove-box as he didn't have much money to his name. He had come across the knife, admired it and knew where and when William had acquired it, as he and his dad had been at the gun show with William. He had slid the knife into the front waistband of his jeans. He had forgotten about it until he felt it digging into his stomach when sprawled over the table after the assault.

"It's fucking Mad Dog's fault," Youngster asserted. "He shouldn't have got the knife then it would never have happened."

Youngster knew this was nonsense but didn't want to acknowledge responsibility; that would mean facing up to the consequences of him killing of Mr Aggressive.

"Fucking Mad Dog!"

Youngster's anger developed into a blame rage. He started cursing William for leaving the house and leaving him there on his own.

Don't go anywhere, he had been told.

What was he was supposed to do, wait and do nothing until fucking Mad Dog decided to come back.

Who does fucking Mad Dog think he is anyway. Fucking Mad Dog can't tell me what to do, he's not my dad.

Youngster didn't listen to his dad either. Why should he? His dad was only thirteen years older than himself. What does his dad know that he doesn't also know?

Youngster embarked on a destructive train of thought, meaning that he wasn't thinking clearly, though recent events showed that he wasn't given to clear thinking.

Fuck Mad Dog, fuck my dad, fuck everyone.

He wasn't going to sit around in this house waiting. He would see Melody and, with that decision made, he picked up the house phone to call his girlfriend. No answer! He then called his friend Pepper, known as such for his love of all food Mexican. Pepper wasn't at home but his mother was there.

"I'll come and pick you up," she said.

Half an hour later Youngster was telling Maria, Pepper's mother, what had happened. Maria had a soft spot for Youngster and not in a motherly way. She stroked his head and held her hand on his cheek. Youngster felt safe. She smiled at him as she leant in to kiss him. Within seconds there was a scramble to reach the bedroom, undressing to save time once there. Youngster was happy to try anything that meant he could forget about earlier events.

They didn't hear the door slam and Pedro, Maria's newest husband, come into the room. The first they knew of his presence was when he pulled Youngster up by his leg off Pedro's wife. Youngster scrambled to sit up but Maria didn't move.

"You little fucker, you're not fit to be let out anywhere. It's all over the streets what you did down at Starbucks. Get your fucking clothes on and get out, and stay away from my wife."

After Youngster had left, Pedro picked up the phone and called the cops to tell them about Youngster.

Youngster was walking down the street dwelling on his spate of bad luck. He hadn't been able to finish what he and Maria had started. He was cursing Pedro, cursing William, cursing his dad and bemoaning his bad luck generally. He didn't hear the car pull up alongside him. The first he was aware was when Officer Tubbs jumped out of the passenger seat and pulled a gun on him.

"Youngster, get down on the ground, don't make me have to shoot you," ordered Officer Tubbs.

Youngster looked at the officer in a daze, then complied. Youngster couldn't believe his bad luck. Why was he being arrested? He hadn't done anything and surely they couldn't have found out it was him who argued with Mr Aggressive.

Of course they had.

Officer Tubbs had received the call to pick up Youngster. He had been in the area, had been taking statements about a daylight robbery at the gas station down the road. Driving up the street, his partner, Officer Garcia, had spotted what he thought was Youngster. They decided stealth was the best approach and the sirens stayed silent; the right decision as the arrest couldn't have gone more smoothly and to plan. The boy looked shaken and dazed and didn't look lucid. Officer Tubbs had seen the look before, in others he had arrested for violent crimes. It wasn't so much the crime they had committed, more that they had been found so speedily that caused the consternation. This boy hadn't fully registered what was going on.

Away with the fairies was Officer Tubbs thought.

4

William had finished his pizza and drunk a couple more beers. For a while, he had cleared his mind of what had happened and it helped him to think clearly, focus on what needed to be done. Finally he stood, cleared up the mess he had made, gave Lenny a call to say he was on his way over to him, then left the house. He drove his Ford truck out of the garage, making sure to lock his garage securely. He had put industrial sized locks and bolts on all his doors including the garage. He didn't want others breaking into his property, like he did to other people's. He jumped into the truck and left. William's house was in the suburbs so it took a time to drive into town and to Lenny's house. He finally pulled into Lenny's driveway alongside a classic Harley Davidson they had recently restored. Another was in Lenny's garage that would be William's, when they'd finished revitalising it. He jumped out of the truck and took a moment to admire the bike before marching into the house. Lenny was seated at the kitchen table cleaning springs and coils from William's bike to be. He was surrounded by beer cans, some empty, but more full.

"What are we going to do about the little fucker." William asked. "We'll have to get him out of town, preferably out of state for his own good. Have you heard from him."

"Not yet," replied Lenny.

At that moment the phone rang.

"Dad, I've been arrested, they're saying they are charging me with murder. What do I do?"

Lenny could hear fear and desperation in his son's voice and needed to reassure him.

"Hang tight son, I'm sending you a lawyer. Don't tell those mother-fuckers anything, not one word. Say nothing! I'll come and see you as soon as I can."

Lenny turned to William. "Well he's out of the frying pan now and into the fire ."

William could see that his best friend was shaken by all that had happened in a short space of time. Lenny and Youngster had always been close, helped by the thirteen year age gap between them. Youngster's mother had left them both when Youngster was three years old. Although five years older than Lenny, she hadn't wanted to be tied down with a kid, so one day she left Lenny a note telling him goodbye and never returned. Neither of heard from her again and Lenny had been upset at the time but, being the pragmatic type, had focussed on raising and providing for his son, whatever way necessary.

"I'll give Smiler a call, he's the best damned attorney there is."

Lenny nodded in agreement and handed the phone over to William. William knew the number by heart, had called Smiler often over the years, the attorney of choice for the outlaw and criminal fraternity. He had certainly negotiated William extremely good deals whenever he'd appeared in court, and had kept him out of prison. The lawyer had acquired the nickname Smiler because he beamed with pleasure at the prosecution when he had beaten them in court, which was more often than not. If he lost a case, he would also smile at them and tell them 'next time'!

"He's on his way down to the jail as we speak," said William. "Come on we need to go and get the cash we need to pay Smiler. I've got two kilos of Ice stashed."

"I've got a kilo of black tar heroin. I took it as payment for a bike."

"Good deal," said William approvingly.

"Right you little fucker, you're being charged with murder, that's your ass spending the rest of your life in prison. Spill your guts now and make it easier on yourself, it can only go downhill for you from here. Why did you do it?"

Sergeant Thomas considered himself a bad-ass, and thought it his mission to bully, threaten and coerce a suspect into a confession, any confession, he didn't care, but the sooner the better. The sergeant was under investigation for dozens of cases of threatening suspects and fabricating confessions.

He looked at Youngster from head to toe and back up again, slowly enough to make Youngster feel the pressure. Youngster shifted uncomfortably in his chair and glanced away. He tried to concentrate on the floor or his fingernails or the chip in the table. Thomas smiled.

It was so easy with most people.

"Come on boy, you know you don't have a choice. You are going to tell me what I want to hear one way or another. May as well unburden yourself now, you'll feel better," Thomas coaxed.

Youngster's facial expressions gave away what he was thinking and feeling. He replayed what he had done a few hours ago and Thomas could read the expressions only too well: fear, anger, worry, insecurity, resolve, rising panic. He loved to see them crumble, the feeling of power that he could inflict this on people. He loved the thrill of intimidating and breaking people to the point of despair until he achieved what he wanted: a confession. He didn't care about the confession and what it was. In his view, whatever they confirmed, under duress or not, they were guilty. He could see that Youngster was about to spill his guts.

"My dad told me not to say anything until I see my attorney," said Youngster, his voice feeble.

There was nothing that made Thomas more infuriated than mention of attorneys and it sent him into a rage.

"Attorneys can't help you where you're going," he derided. "All they're good for is putting cash in their pockets. None of them are interested in helping a snivelly low life like you."

He didn't see or hear the door open behind him. He was too fixated on terrorising Youngster.

"You worthless little mother-fucker, an attorney isn't going to keep you out of prison, you little punk murderer," Thomas bellowed in his face.

He hoisted Youngster out of his chair by his t-shirt and slammed him against the wall. The t-shirt being too flimsy to hold Youngster's weight meant that he inevitably slid down the wall. As he crumpled, Thomas gave him a kick in his ribcage then held his arm and twisted it so that Youngster had no choice but to turn around. He found himself face down with his nose almost touching the dirty concrete. He screamed with pain as he felt his arm forced up his back, but there was no release of tension only more pain.

"Sergeant Thomas," bellowed Smiler. "Put my client down and leave. I will be pressing charges against you again later."

Officer Hernandez who had escorted Smiler to the interview room looked down at the floor making sure to avert her gaze from what she'd witnessed for she was scared to death of Thomas. He made the workplace miserable not just for her but many of the other female officers with his condescending chauvinism, incessant sexual innuendos towards them or conversely insults about the way they looked. She hadn't signed up for this but there was no support from her superiors. The general attitude was, "if you can't hack it there's the door".

Thomas dropped Youngster and smiled as he looked round at the voice.

"Smiler, it's always good to see you. You always know how to spoil my fun."

Smiler gave Thomas a dazzling smile but didn't reply to the comment. "See you later Sergeant."

He stood aside to let Thomas out of the room.

"Come on Hernandez, you can give me some head at my desk." He took her arm and pulled her along.

Officer Hernandez didn't know whether to be appalled or petrified and she did an excellent impression of both.

"Officer Hernandez," called out Smiler, "if he lays one inappropriate finger on you or makes any more lewd suggestions let me know. I will sue his ass. It's my mission to get him fired!"

Officer Hernandez looked at Smiler and gave him a weak but grateful smile. Thomas continued walking composed, in a rare display of self control.

Smiler shut the door and turned to Youngster who was now back in his seat and nursing his arm. His breathing was laboured and rasping.

"Do you need to get that seen to," Smiler asked.

"I don't know, it really hurts, and it hurts where he kicked me." He pulled up his t-shirt and showed Smiler the big red swollen area on his ribcage.

Smiler stood up, stuck his head out of the door and shouted at the room. "Get me an ambulance here now."

He turned back to Youngster. "Ok, while we wait for the ambulance, tell me what's going on. Mad dog called and said to get down here right away."

Youngster told him everything that had happened. When he finished talking he started to cry.

"Ok Youngster, don't worry. First things first. Let's get you checked out at the hospital. Then I'll file charges against Thomas for assault."

The ambulance arrived and the paramedics stretchered Youngster away as a precaution. They were certain he had at least one broken rib. He was accompanied by Officer Hernandez who was relieved to leave the building and away from the firing line of Thomas and his cronies.

6

Youngster eventually went to trial and received a twenty two year sentence with a requirement to serve fifty percent before parole would be considered. His family had rallied round and raised the money needed for a decent lawyer. This was reflected in his ultimate sentence, different to the forty years, sixty years and life had been rumoured.

Under negative influences of other young inmates, and older inmates with agendas, Youngster thrived in prison. He ignored and bucked the system, broke any and all rules as often as he could and, when he discovered by the prison guards he spent the time in segregation, annoying older and hardened inmates with his antics.

He would go to the outside enclosed recreation yard, shimmy up the metal pole and walk across the steel girder supporting the pavilion roof, banging on the panels as he balanced on it's narrow width. He would look down at the spectators, laughing as he joked around, pretending to slip and fall. Many of the younger inmates would shout encouragement at his endless antics, but the older ones were displeased, fearful that he would bring the law to their doors.

One time, Youngster had scaled the 20 feet high wire fencing to retrieve a basketball which had become lodged between terminating coils of razor wire that sent out a vicious reminder that there was no escape. Being small and wiry, it had been easy for him to climb up, like a squirrel running up a tree. He perched his small frame in-between the coils of miniature blades which would rip to shreds anything that came into contact with them, and extricated the ball. He was oblivious to the guard in the tower shouting dire warnings at him to come down or he would be shot. He didn't spot the rifle pointed at him in readiness should he decide to drop down the other side. The inmates on the ground backed away from the fence; they wanted no part of being shot. That escapade earned him ninety days in segregation.

Youngster also created a unique hustle for himself. He would bet willing inmates - of which there was an endless supply - ten dollars that he could jump off three row and land without hurting himself. When someone took him on, he would climb on the top rail and jump off. It didn't faze him that the height was over twenty five feet, not thinking about it. He would adopt a crouch position and land with bent knees. As soon as his feet touched the ground he went into a roll across the concrete floor. He then leapt up, bounded over to the inmate who took the bet and ordered them to pay up. It was a great source of amusement for those in the day room.

Youngster had been play fighting with his cellie one day, another hot-head who irritated many of the older inmates. He was part of a black gang and they had shown their displeasure at him for being friendly with his white cellie, but all their warnings had fallen on deaf ears. They had started their tussle in the cell, then moved out onto the run to give themselves more space. Youngster and his cellie had been at it for half an hour and the other guys were fed up of having to jump out of their way. The play fighting paused as they took a rest and leant against the railing and Youngster climbed up to sit on it. As usual he couldn't stay still and kicked out at his cellie, who in turn caught hold of his foot to stop him. Youngster lost his balance on the railing and, as he pulled his leg away to steady himself, tumbled backwards. Unable to save himself, he screamed in panic. The blood-curdling sound was cut short as his head smashed against the corner of the floor on his way down. When he hit the ground, Youngster was dead.

William's trial was held several months before that of Youngster's, before it had been proven that a murder had occurred.

He was charged and convicted of "Party to Murder" under the offence "Law of Parties". Whilst this law was not unique to Texas, the state used it prolificly to achieve long sentences for the litigant, no matter how tenuous the involvement.

As Youngster hadn't entered a plea and was taking his case to trial, his lawyer wouldn't allow him to testify at William's trial in his defence.

The prosecuting attorney hated William from previous encounters and was determined to incarcerate him for good. The Judge's refusal to allow material evidence vital to the case, Youngster's absence as a witness and Melody's poor performance whilst high from an unknown substance on the stand ensured that the prosecution had an easy job of finding William guilty. The poor performance from his public defender, who had limited experience in murder trials, compounded William's rail-roading.

His wife at the time had promised to retain a good lawyer as Smiler had died two months prior to the trial, so was unavailable. Instead, she sold the house he'd built along with his classic weaponry collection, his vehicles and anything else she could sell. She moved to another state, leaving him high and dry and at the mercy of a public defender and a system that cared little for justice, only mass incarceration.

William was handed a seventy five year sentence and, on appeal, his conviction was overturned on a technicality. William rattled around in prison for the six years it took for the prosecutor to fulfil his mission of keeping him behind bars until the prosecutor managed to have his conviction overturned again, keeping him in prison. He had no money or external support to his fight.

William had been in prison for nine years.

William made one last check of the wine he had spent the past five days brewing and tried a mouthful to check it was ready for consumption. He had spent almost every day of the past nine years drunk. A shudder went through William's body and his face contorted as the unsophisticated potion hit his taste buds. He had the well earned reputation of making the best wine in the unit, had at least three five gallon batches on the go at any time and used different hiding places for each one. Sometimes concealed in the kitchen or laundry, often in different cells, occasionally the craft shop, and, when the need arose, in mattresses. This time the concoction was hidden behind the toilet in Lenny's cell. Lenny had been stealing extra supplies from the kitchen to make a batch of wine for Angel's thirtieth birthday, a milestone age in prison for guys who had been living criminal lives, violence and death more the norm. William had been surprised when he had reached the big three O. None of his family expected it either and he'd been hearing since his tenth birthday that he'd be dead by the age of fifteen, eighteen, twenty five. He smiled wryly to himself, happy that he had proven those losers wrong so often.

Four of the inmates were going to have a big spread for dinner, a surprise for Angel who didn't think anyone knew that it was his birthday. They had all contributed different food items; William had collected cookies and traded some of them for chocolate, sweets and candies to make a birthday cake for Angel. William had planned in advance for this and paid someone to bring in candles to decorate the cake.

When the day arrived, they ate a feast of Tortilla chips smothered in chilli with rice, pickles and jalapeño peppers and a generous sprinkling of grated cheese stolen from the kitchen. Roast beef, mashed potato, more cheese, pickles and peppers chopped up, with ranch dressing and crushed chips had been placed on top . This was washed down with cans of coke followed by chocolate cheesecake made from crushed cookies, cream cheese and snickers bars. Angel was overwhelmed and further stunned at thirty small candles decorating in his cake, the flames threatening to burn his eyebrows when he bent to blow them out.

Joining their little party were Angel's right and left hand men, Carlos One and Carlos Two their nicknames. A few of William's associates from his gang were present, all guys he'd grown up with on the streets and had known for years. He wouldn't have trusted them as individuals but, as members of the same gang, he knew he could count on them to support him and back him up in prison, whatever occurred.

William had joined a gang on his second visit to prison. After his release from his two year stint as a minor, he had stayed free for a mere thirty three days, racking up forty seven felonies ranging from burglary of a habitation and strong-arm robbery to possession of heroin under one gramme. There had been some killings but the law didn't know about those and, in William's opinion, were all deserved. Smiler had been his attorney for all of his charges.

Joining the gang had served him well for his last three stints in prison. William had served two years for a murder he had committed as a child, then a twelve year sentence for a string of burglaries and home invasions, of which he served one year, plus an eight year sentence in federal prison where he spent six years in an isolation cell speaking to nobody, seeing only an officer - minus small talk - when his food tray was delivered.

He had joined one of the white gangs, a small organisation. They would do the dirty work of larger white gangs, and back them up during fights and their 'wars'. These were long-standing gangs such as the Aryan Brotherhood, Aryan Circle, Aryan Nation, White Knights and Peckerwood Mafia. The gang had grown rapidly in the prison system since it had been formed in a Texas unit in 1989. After joining, William's time in prison had been made easier, albeit drama filled. A few guys he'd grown up around had convinced William to join and, he saw it as an opportunity to watch each others back, more mutual camaraderie and friendship than any belief system the gangs held, which often didn't hold up to scrutiny.

Because of his willingness to fight and rarely being beaten, plus an ability to think strategically, he moved up the ranks, learning the rules and mission statement by heart and strictly adhering to them. He held others accountable when they didn't pass the muster, always considered the go-to guy. But, he was much more perceptive and calculating than others, could tell what was going on wherever he was present. He was tuned into the atmosphere, sensing the tensions, accurately predicting when a riot would kick off, where it would start, and who would be the instigators. William considered this prudent, part of a necessary set of survival skills. surprised at how few inmates had developed those keen senses. He had developed the same instincts as a child living on the streets. Had he not, he would be dead, as so many others were.

ℓ

William had been released from segregation after spending two years there. He had been given multiple major cases for assaults against officers, usually whilst restrained after fights. Segregation didn't bother William, it just served to hone his skills of sign language, passing and receiving items using a line under the door, writing kite and solidifying his reputation.

Being locked in the cell for twenty three hours a day had little impact on his well-being unlike most guys who couldn't handle isolation. On a previous stint in federal prison, he had spent six years in an isolation cell where he had no human contact for the duration of his segregation time. Nothing to keep him occupied like writing a letter, although he had received a letter which had then been projected up onto the wall of his cell to be read. He had read an occasional book when one was pushed through his hatch and had spent his time exercising, improving his fitness and strength. For William, it was essential to have a strong mind and keep it occupied, otherwise, within weeks, psychological problems would haunt him. Many an inmate had become crazy from the isolation but he had emerged from that experience unscathed, except that he was meaner. By comparison with the Federal sort, segregation in a state prison was a walk in the park.

William could shower when he wanted as it was located in the cell and he didn't have to share his space with dozens of other men, instead focusing on a workout regime. A bonus was that he didn't have to cope with the morons who were the staple of prison life. He took pleasure in making the officers do his bidding in segregation as everything had to be done by them and he needed to be escorted everywhere. This was his five star hotel and he could work on cementing his relationships with the chiefs of the cartels and gangs he had worked with, running drugs across country for several of them whilst out in the free world. They had been good to him and paid well for his services. In solitary confinement, he didn't have to worry about his property or commissary being stolen. The officers who worked in segregation tended to be more relaxed than the general prison guard population, a policy decision; because of the harsh conditions of segregation it was necessary to keep everyone calm. Often, the same officers had worked seg for years as other officers found they couldn't handle it, too volatile or not mentally weak.

The first person William spotted when he walked through the door of his new section was Lenny. He wasn't surprised to see him, although he hadn't known he was back in prison. Lenny was squaring up to a much larger black man who was labouring under the misapprehension that he controlled both televisions in the day room. Lenny was making it clear that he didn't care about the one near the officers' desk but the other TV is not being controlled by any black man whose cell isn't anywhere near it. William strode over to where they were arguing and dropped his belongings.

The big black man glanced over at him.

"Fuck off, what do you want?"

"I'm changing the channel on the TV," William said as he jumped up on the metal stool to stand on the table to reach the controls.

"Don't fucking touch that. I say what channel it goes on and it stays on sport," asserted Mighty Mouth.

"Not any more you don't. We do. Now fuck off back to your side of the room," ordered William.

This sent the guy into a rage but, before he could do anything, William, from his position on top of the table, had kicked him in the centre of his chest, the thud audible as boot met flesh. The force sent the man stumbling across the room before he stopped, steadying himself using another table. He stood, ready to retaliate but William had already jumped to the floor and was close enough for his antagonist to see how sharp was the blade of William's home-made shank. Wisely, the inmate chose to retreat and crawled back to his cell.

"Fuck's sake Lenny, it seems I spend my whole life saving you," William joked.

"It's what you were put on this earth for you fat mother fucker," Lenny replied as they gave each other a bear hug.

They laughed and reminisced about old times, talking about Lenny's son, Youngster, who had been keeping his nose clean under the guidance of Lenny's former weekly visits and his fellow gang members keeping their eyes on him. He was unaware of how his son would fare now that Lenny was back in prison and they were housed in units on opposite sides of the state. The mood had become sombre so they lightened it by talking about the last time they had seen each other.

9

Lenny had just scored a nice load of boy and was seated in his car as he mixed a dose and injected it into a vein. He fired up his old Chevy truck and set off, heading to the lake to meet Mad Dog and some of the other guys for a beer and barbecue party for a birthday party. Driving along the lake road, he smiled as he thought of swimming in the lake and imbibing until he was drunk. As he was driving he started to nod out, shaking his head increasingly violently to try to clear his vision and stay awake.

Too late he saw the sharp bend in the road.

William and Baldy saw Lenny leave the road at Graveyard Gully, a notorious black spot for cars running over the edge. They stared down at the old Chevy truck lying on it's roof twenty metres down the hillside, lodged front end in a tree, its size and maturity ensuring that it remained immovable. They could see Lenny, arm hanging out of the open window and jumped out of the truck and ran down the hillside. Baldy opened the door of the Chevy as William grabbed hold of Lenny under his arms to pull him away from the vehicle. After some manoeuvring around the displaced steering wheel they finally pulled Lenny free of the vehicle and Lenny opened his eyes as he was being dragged from his vehicle by William. He nodded out again straight away.

"Fucking stupid bastard, wake up and help us get you out," cursed William as he gave Lenny a kick on his thigh.

Lenny lay in the grass moaning and dribbling but remained unconscious. William kicked him a couple more times out of frustration.

"We need to get away from here before the cops come by," William said. "they are up and down here all the time."

"Pour some beer over his face," suggested Baldy, so named for suffering alopecia his whole life leaving him with patches of wispy hair.

"Are you fucking crazy. I'm not wasting good beer on this mother-fucker," objected William.

He gave Lenny a couple of open hand slaps on the face but the only response from him was an incoherent mumble and a dribble of drool from the corner of his mouth. William and Baldy each took hold of an arm and dragged Lenny up the hillside. Although Lenny was small he was a dead weight whilst asleep and the uneven terrain made hauling him up the incline difficult.

"Fuck it," declared William as he pulled a can of beer out of his pocket, tugged on the ring tab off and poured the golden brown liquid onto Lenny's face.

Lenny spluttered as the ale ran up his nose, into his mouth and down his throat. He opened his eyes and looked at William and Baldy in surprise. He looked around him and saw his truck lodged in the tree.

"Oh fuck, I must have nodded out.," he said, then added, groggily, "We need to get my truck towed back up the hill."

"Fuck that," said William. "My truck won't pull that back up to the road, and it's totalled anyway. Let's just get out of here before the cops turn up."

"Fuck, that was a good truck," declared Lenny. "Ok. Get me out of here and give me a beer."

William and Baldy had to help Lenny get back up to the road and into William's truck, his knees buckling as he drifted, losing consciousness.

William had been arrested a week later for his part in Mr Aggressive's murder, after leading the police a merry chase all over town for several days. He was initially stopped by a patrol car for having a tail light out on his latest set of wheels, a black Mustang with a souped up engine he had taken in exchange for wiping out a drug debt.

When asked for his driving licence William knew he was in trouble. First, because he didn't have a driving licence. Second, because he was already on parole. Third, he knew there was an APB (all points bulletin) out for him for his part in the murder of Mr Aggressive. William had made the decision not to give up easily and informed the officer that he had no licence, then slammed the car into gear and took off, leaving the officer standing in a cloud of dust. William looked in his rear-view mirror and saw the officer dash back to his car and speak urgently into his radio, then jump into his car and give chase. Within minutes he heard and then saw the police helicopter flying low across the sky. It was obvious that it was seeking him when it circled close to his location. When he heard multiple sirens from police cars closing in, it confirmed his suspicions. Now that the helicopter had pinged him he needed to keep moving but he was about to drive into rush hour traffic stopped ahead at the traffic lights. He had to do something and fast; traffic was building up. He performed an immediate U-turn onto the other side other the road, over-revving the engine causing the tyres to squeal. Keeping control, William raced down the way he had driven. With a grin decorating his face, he watched three squad cars slow, assess the situation and drive a hundred yards further before being able to turn at the traffic lights to resume their pursuit. He led them a merry chase for a few miles but the police cars maintained their distance behind him, not yet closing in on him. He knew they had a strategy in play and it wasn't his first police pursuit. He was certain of their next move and, in confirmation, he saw another vehicle, lights flashing, at the side of the road, an officer next to it, ready to roll out the road spikes at just the right moment. Another officer, gun in hand, was ready for the moment the spikes shredded the tyres and the pursuit car came to an enforced stop. William was ready for the move and timed his manoeuvre perfectly. As the officer stepped forward to roll the spikes, he pulled the wheel sharp to the right and drove at speed up the grass banking, brown and parched from the extreme summer heat. The Mustang held traction on the steep sided verge. As he rejoined the road a short way ahead, he didn't need to check his mirror to know one of the cop cars hadn't stopped in time to avoid the spikes. He heard the noise of tyres exploding and laughed raucously as he put his foot down further. Once the spikes were removed, two of the cars continued their chase, as did the helicopter.

William decided more extreme measures needed to be taken and, never one to do things half-heartedly, he raced towards the interstate. The cop cars were taking it in turns to try to pass him, to no avail. The officers surmised that he was heading for the interstate and were determined to stop him before he could do that. They were again surprised by William's move when he made it look like he was entering the slip road, but a late manoeuvre saw him change tack. Instead, he drove down the exit ramp giving the oncoming traffic a shock with many of the drivers taking measures to avoid a perceived collision. The squad cars came to an abrupt halt, failing to follow William onto the interstate, deemed it too dangerous to conduct a pursuit travelling the wrong way down a four lane carriageway at speed. In these instances it was policy to abandon the chase and William was fully cognizant with this fact, which was why he chose that course of action. He drove down the shoulder to the next entrance ramp, weaving his way up to exit the interstate to a volley of car horns. Once he was no longer causing a danger to other drivers the helicopter pulled away and William was left to make his way to somewhere safe.

The following day William received numerous phone calls from friends and acquaintances, telling him that the cops had been to their house looking for him, offering generous cash payments for information leading to his arrest. Later that evening, a news item on the local television and radio stations offered a substantial reward to anyone providing information that led to William being caught. A few days later, flyers and business cards appeared. and his face, name, aliases and details of the alleged crime were distributed in all the areas of the city he was known to frequent. His wife was visited at her home and place of work to find out what she knew, which was nothing. William had been careful never to tell her anything he was doing, then she could tell the cops nothing. She would call him and say he should turn himself in and he would tell her she was crazy and hang up. On one occasion, she arranged to meet him for dinner but he suspected he was being set up. He was proven correct when he arrived early and watched as a two plain clothes cops went in the restaurant and made out to be a couple of diners. He watched his wife step out of the new truck he had recently bought her and called her phone.

"I didn't realise you wanted rid of me so badly, bitch," he said.

"What do you mean," she asked as she looked guiltily around.

"Don't play dumb. Setting me up for the cops to get me. Will you be getting the reward money too?" he asked.

He hadn't thought she would stoop so low as to snitch on her own husband but things between them hadn't been good for a long time; this was even worse than he had imagined. He'd forgiven her for countless affairs she'd over the years, particularly when he was serving stints in prison, even let it go over his head when she preached at him at how she was committed to her marriage. Snitching, he couldn't forgive, it was the ultimate sin. The cops would use sneaky and dirty tactics, he knew, but it was now clear to William that she had been interested in him for what she could make from him, William being generous to those in his life, that was plenty. She was just like all the other hanger-ons he provided for when he had money.

A couple of days later William went to deposit money in the drive-thru facility of his bank. No human contact was involved with the transaction but the drive-thru stations were covered by CCTV which were monitored inside the bank. A teller looked at the screen and spotted William's face. She didn't know him, as such, but they had been to the same school years before, albeit in different classes. She left her station and went to speak to the manager who called the police. William finished his banking and set off towards the exit but didn't make it. A police car screeched to a stop across the exit, and another one raced into the entrance, blocking William from behind.

William didn't react. He knew when the game was up and stayed in the car, waiting for the cops to come to him. Four officers jumped out of the vehicles, guns drawn and trained on the car. William wound the window down.

"Well it took you a while but you got me," he grinned.

"You didn't exactly make it easy for us," Officer One replied, laughing. "We thought we had you with the road spikes but that stunt you pulled was straight out of the movies."

"You're all so predictable, it's fun beating you at your own game," William said.

"Predictable as we are, you know the routine. Get out of the car, put your hands against it and spread your feet apart."

16

Lenny picked up William's mattress at the same time William picked up his property. They went over to his allocated cell on one row, called to the officer to open the cell and he got his property organised. After making his bed, William leant against the top bunk whilst Lenny cleaned his locker. There was a young Mexican sitting cross-legged on the top bunk. It was evident to both Lenny and William that this boy had a huge chip on his shoulder and a bad attitude to boot.

Spider, so called because of the spiders' web tattoos he had on elbows, knees and the back of his shaven head, looked at them both And snarled, "You mother-fuckers are disturbing me. You, you fat fucker get off my bed."

William and Lenny looked at each other but didn't say a word. William took his arm off Spider's bunk, finished arranging his property in the storage box and his commissary items in his locker then they both left the cell. They went back to the day room and sat at an empty table and laughed as they stared at each other.

"I think I'll be having some fun later," predicted William.

A couple of hours later William went back to his cell. Spider was laid on his bunk. When William came in Spider jumped down and pointed his finger in William's face.

"This is my cell and my rules asshole. I decide when you can come back in and have alone time. If you don't like my rules, fuck off. The floor needs cleaning, make sure you've done that when I come back."

Again William looked at Spider, saying nothing, biding his time until he could teach this badass a lesson, in a place and time of his choosing. William allowed no one to control him and certainly not some young punk. William ensured that everything he did was for his own benefit. Spider pushed his way past him and stalked off to the day room.

William stood in the doorway of his cell watching what was happening in the day room, paying particular attention to Spider. It was never wasted time watching the activities, the body language and behaviour of others; any information he gathered would come in useful, even even save his life.

Spider stomped over to one of the tables where four old men were seated. He was in a foul mood, how dare they give him a cellie, let alone one from another race. He had made it clear to the officers that he liked to be alone or at least to choose his cellie.

"You," he pointed at a small grey haired man using a crutch to walk. "I want cookies and coke. Give me cookies and coke, and some soups for later."

"Fuck off, buy your own," retorted the old man, barely giving Spider a glance.

Spider's face contorted in fury at this response and he grabbed the shoulder of the shrivelled black man and yanked him backwards. Inevitably the old guy fell off the stool and Spider put his booted foot on the old man's chest.

"Listen old man, you are nothing. When I fucking tell you to jump, you ask how fucking high." He didn't wait for a response, assuming that he'd put enough fear into each of the oldies to make them do as he told them from now on.

None of the other elderly men around the table were capable of standing up to this obnoxious youngster and were not looking for conflict or any repercussions from disobeying Spider's demands.

They muttered amongst themselves, then took some unopened packs of cookies plus a couple of cans of coke they had collectively contributed to the table and handed them to him. Spider snatched the goodies from their hands, peered at the cookies in disgust and told them to buy different cookies next time, and chocolate bars.

William watched with interest. He had the measure of Spider as soon as he first saw him in the cell - a bully - but William hadn't wanted to expose anything of himself at that point. William looked up at two and three row to see if he recognised anyone. He spotted Angel, a Mexican he knew well from his neighbourhood, having done several jobs transporting tens of kilos of cocaine across country for Angel's father and uncle, both top members of the Mexican Mafia. William had helped Angel's wife and children financially to set them up in a new city after Angel had been convicted of murdering a competing drug trafficker while his rival was trying to rob him. Angel had not wanted his family involved in cartel life, now that he wasn't there to protect them in person.

Angel had watched Spider's little drama too but he had seen it before. William strolled up the stairs to talk to him.

"Hey Mad Dog it's been a while," he greeted William with genuine pleasure.

"Who is that little fucker?" William asked. "He's my cellie. Seems to think he runs things, but he's about to find out different."

"Remember the guy I killed? It's his nephew. He's the son of his sister. Remember her? She was meaner than anyone I've ever known. Anyway he's in for a ten stretch for robbing another rival dealer. It obviously runs in the family." Angel sniggered.

Lenny who was also housed on three row sauntered along when he saw William and Angel talking. They each watched Spider pin a Hispanic youngster against the wall for not possessing anything that he wanted.

"Time to take care of the little bastard. Angel can you get him up here?"

"No problem, this is going to be fun," he chuckled.

William and Lenny stepped back into Angel's cell to stay out of sight.

"Hey Spider," called out Angel. "I've got some fried chicken you can have. Come and get it."

Spider looked up to see who was talking . He had traded items with Angel before and considered him to be kosher but he was unaware that Angel had killed his uncle. Spider took the stairs two at a time.

"What else have you got?"

As he was speaking, William and Lenny stepped out. Quick as a flash, William grabbed Spider by the back of his shirt collar and the back of his waistband, picked him up, spun round and slammed him against the wall, all in a series of fluid movements. Spider yelped in surprise, then fury, as he realised what was happening. He couldn't move and it hurt when he tried. His shirt was strangling him and his trousers were wedged so far up his crack that it felt like his genitals were being garrotted.

"Just to make things clear, my fucking cell my fucking rules. What I say goes. If you don't like it fuck off and ask to be moved. I don't give a fuck either way." As William said this he pulled Spider's waistband higher. "Am I making myself understood?"

"Yes, let me down. Whatever you say."

Spider was shocked, he wasn't used to being challenged. He had always had the back-up and protection of his wider family growing up, and was taught go in fast, mean and aggressive. People will comply, they told him.

William looked at Lenny and Angel. They both shrugged as William let go of Spider and he crumpled at the knees as his feet touched the concrete again. William stepped back as Spider smoothed himself down.

"Fuck you old man," he spat at William.

William simulated a pained expression on his face and a demeanour suggesting he was disappointed in his young charges' behaviour. Spider had backed up towards the railing as he hurled insults at William. William stepped forward and pushed Spider against and over the railing. Sliding over the top, Spider felt himself falling head first over the other side until William grabbed hold of his left leg. Lenny jumped forward and gripped Spider's right leg and Angel stood to the side leaning on the railings enjoying the entertainment.

Spider screamed in terror at the thought of falling head first onto the concrete. That would be the end of him.

"Let me up mother-fuckers," he screamed in panic.

At the commotion, everyone looked up to see what was going on. As in-and-out was taking place, those in their cells exited to see what was happening. They jeered, clapped and laughed at this unexpected entertainment, with TV forgotten for the moment.

"Mad dog, you crazy mother-fucker, let him go," shouted Officer Stead who walked in just as Spider screamed.

"Whatever you say boss," William replied with a grin on his face and he and Lenny each loosened their hold on Spider's legs. An even more panicked scream emanated from Spider as he felt himself fall what felt like several feet, though, in reality, only a couple of inches.

"Mad dog, do not let him go! Pull the little fucker back up," ordered Stead. "I do not want to have to deal with the paperwork when you drop him."

"Are you sure boss, you don't look like you're doing much. It'll keep you busy."

There was a burst of laughter from the day room at this exchange.

"Mad dog, I'm warning you..."

"Ok boss whatever you say. No need to get your panties in a wad."

Officer Stead stood with his hands on his hips and shaking his head. *That fucking Mad dog!*

"Is there something you want to say?" William asked Spider.

Spider didn't answer, he was too busy crying.

"Who runs things here?" William asked him.

"You do," snivelled Spider.

"Glad we got things sorted out," William said as they pulled Spider back over the railings and deposited him on the floor.

11

William had gone to chow and watched the room to see what was going on. At the same time he was listening to the chatter going on around him.

"Hey punk," he heard a voice say in front of him. "When are you going to give me some head? I see you giving it out freely all over the unit."

"You'll have to ask my man about that," replied Whisper, so called because he was very soft spoken.

"Why the fuck should I do that. Maybe I'll just take me some anyway."

William had looked round to see who was talking, and saw an average height, lean black man with gold grills on his teeth. He didn't recognise either of them as they lived on a different pod to him. William looked straight at Goldie, who looked back and smirked.

"Maybe I'll fuck both you white boys in the ass, and make you like it," he chuckled.

William stared at him long and hard to take in his features and mannerisms so that he would remember him. There wasn't much to distinguish him from any average black man other than his ridiculous gold teeth except for a small scar, pretty old, probably from childhood, just above his left eyebrow. He also had half a finger missing on his right hand, the middle finger had the section from the bottom knuckle missing, making it shorter than his other fingers. William said nothing but was plotting in his head how to retaliate; he would bide his time.

12

Two new laws walked on the pod accompanied by Officer Stead, one a petite white female who didn't look old enough to have finished school, and an equally small but rotund white guy in his early twenties who looked scared to death. Everyone occupying the day room stared as they walked through the door. Then the shouting, jeering and abuse started, with the bolder inmates walking behind the new boots and pinching them on the bum.

"Mad dog, shut the fuck up, can't you see they're still wet behind the ears. You'll scare them if you're not careful," said Officer Stead with a cheeky twinkle in his eyes.

William laughed and sat back whilst others made all manner of crude, disparaging and uncomplimentary comments about the new recruits. New officers were always a source of fascination and fun for the inmates and they would size them up. Height, weight, size, expressions and demeanour to see how easy they would be to control, manipulate and coerce. The wages paid to staff were so poor that offers from inmates to make a thousand dollars each month for bringing in two baggies of weed was extremely tempting. More often than not, the chance of extra income overcame officers' common sense and fear of repercussions if or when found out. It didn't seem a big deal. Two baggies, each with a quarter of an ounce of marijuana, in the free world costing twenty five dollars a pack, but inside prison worth four to five hundred dollars. Smuggling into the unit was easy, despite security scanners and pat downs for visitors and staff. To those tempted by free money every month, it represented minimal risk for great rewards.

William had the measure of both youngsters immediately. The girl, Huntley, wore a blank expression on her face with the only give-away, her eyes. William was impressed with her resolve and refusal to feel intimidated. He'd seen it before in other recruits, but it often crumbled once they were left to their own devices on the job. Nevertheless, she wasn't going to be an easy nut to crack.

William liked to see the females do well in the job and hated seeing weaker ones fall for the charms and the lies of inmates, particularly the black men who could be insidious and for whom white women were a trophy. He had always held women in higher regard than men, thanks to the influence of his grandfather. When the ignorant inmates were making their derogatory comments about women, extolling their perceived God given right to control and subjugate women, William would denigrate them and inform them how pathetic they were. He would ask them how they, being miserable and pathetic specimen of men, could believe that they were superior to women. These comments inevitably had the inmates up in arms and William would be subjected to barrages of abuse. Not that he was affected by it in any way and he would laugh at them, enjoying watching them become worked up. William was ambivalent about being popular, preferring being feared, and his 'unique' opinions did nothing to endear him to many inmates or staff.

The young officer, Donovan, was going to be a pushover, unlikely to last long in the job. Faced with the forty eight jeering inmates in his section of the pod had turned him green, on the verge of puking and terror decorated his face. Donovan stood behind one of the tables, as if his personal security barrier, and looked down, careful to resist eye contact with anyone. The animals laughed and made lude comments.

"Come on Donovan, show some balls," said Officer Stead. "Give some of those deadbeats a case for something, anything. Make it up if you like, just show them who's running things around here."

Donovan lurched into action, running as fast as his short legs could take him to the inmates' bathrooms. He ran past William, pushing him out of the way in his quest to reach a toilet to throw up in. William grinned as everyone else jeered and taunted him.

William slid around the corner into the bathroom area after Donovan. He stood in the open doorway of the toilet stall waiting for the rookie to stop retching. When he stood upright and turned around, he found William blocking his way. William smiled at him and asked Donovan if he was feeling alright now. Donovan, were it possible, looked more terrified at being cornered by this bulky inmate who's smile was anything but reassuring.

"How would you like to make extra money to top up your pay cheque?" William asked him.

"How can I do that?" Donovan asked.

"One baggie of weed a week, an extra four hundred a week in your pocket, and for that I'll make sure you're looked after whilst you're working here," offered William.

Donovan lost some of his terror when it seemed that William wasn't about to kill and eat him. He relaxed slightly, enough to give the offer some thought. A friend was working as an officer on another unit and was making a thousand a week doing the same thing. His mate had just bought himself a brand new truck, paid for in cash; he was the one who encouraged Donovan to become a corrections officer, mostly due to the benefits on offer. He thought quickly about the things he could buy with the money he would be making.

William watched the officer's face and knew he had him when Donovan had asked 'how'. William wasn't about to take the guy at face value though, he would have to be tested to see that he was reliable and could be trusted.

"So when are you going to bring the first stash," asked William. He had to make sure to get Donovan on the hook straight away; if he didn't someone else would recruit him and William would have lost his mule.

Donovan looked up at William.

"I didn't realise it would have to be straight away. I thought I'd have time to think about it."

"You've already thought about it, the sooner you start the sooner that cash is in your hand. Plus I can't protect you from the other animals if you're not committed," William coaxed.

Donovan thought about this very quickly. He would certainly like to be protected.

"I can bring some tomorrow," he said, a quaver in his voice suggesting uncertainty.

William dug his hand in his pocket and pulled out a wad of bank notes and Donovan observed that they were all fifties. He wondered how William had access to cash in prison, and at such quantities. He remembered from his training course that cash is a high risk contraband but didn't question, simply opening out his hand when William gave him a fifty.

"Bring two baggies, we'll knock the fifty off your first pay-out."

Donovan pocketed the cash and, on William's asking, told him what shifts he would be on.

"How do I bring it in because there is security?"

"The back door always works well," replied William.

"What back door? I thought we had to come through the main entrance," said Donovan in a puzzled voice.

William looked at him in disbelief. He couldn't possible be this naive, but it appeared he was.

"Put it up in your asshole, asshole. Make sure to use plenty of grease and wrap those baggies well."

Donovan looked appalled as William, quick off the mark, knowing that the rookie's train of thought was backtracking, gave Donovan no time to back out of the deal.

"Right, get back in there and stop being a cowardly mother fucker," William said, as he gave Donovan a shove towards the day room. The whole exchange had only taken a couple of minutes and the inmates were still shouting and jeering, having fun at the new boots' expense. As Donovan walked past them he was pinched on the bum numerous times and each time he would flinch and try to step away, but he was surrounded by his antagonists. Officer Stead watched Donovan come back, closely followed by William, who looked Stead straight in the eyes and smirked.

"He's ok now boss," William said and laughed as he sat on a table at the back of the day room.

"Ok you mother-fuckers have had your fun now, back off and let them leave. Mad Dog, a word."

William walked over to the officer and knew what was coming.

"What word would that be boss. Are you going to tell me or do I need to guess. Will it be a word I know or do I need to get a dictionary?"

"Don't let me find out you smartass mother-fucker..." Stead knew all too well some of the things William was in to and admitted to most of them if asked.

"That was eight words boss, nine if you consider mother-fucker to be two," said William, laughing.

"Fuck off smartass."

Stead turned away and left with the new boots to subject them to more prison realities.

William laughed to himself. He had a lot of time for Stead, known him a long time and knew that he was fair and consistent in his dealings with inmates. You knew where you stood with him, could always have a laugh and joke with the guys but he couldn't be walked over or bought. He rarely issued cases and would try and lose cases written willy-nilly by other power hungry officers, of which there were far too many. He treated inmates like humans and men; in return he demanded respect and it didn't bode well for those who failed to respect him.

William was pleased with the way that transaction had gone, easier than most. Many newcomers didn't want to commit, so were given the spiel of how protection would be beneficial to them. Comply or they would be terrorised and their lives made hell whilst on the unit, forced to participate in sexual activities and certainly beaten up. The naive young officers were often horrified at what might happen to them that they agreed to be mules out of fear and others lasted only a short time in the job. As William knew only too well, they were unreliable, took a lot of coaxing, nurturing and babying; William was never certain that they could be trusted.

It was two days later when Donovan came into the pod again, this time on his own and less nervous than his first time. Having survived the first couple of days on the job unscathed had given him misplaced confidence, even having the nerve to instruct a couple of the guys to back off when they pinched his bum. They chortled but backed off anyway. Progress indeed.

William watched with interest from the door of his cell where he stayed until Donovan came to him. In too obvious manner, that attracted the attention of a collection of inmates seated round a table eating, Donovan walked up to William. The inmates watched as Donovan gave William something,. William whispered in the officer's ear that he needed to be more discreet and Donovan walked away sheepishly.

"Hey Donovan," called William.

Donovan turned around and walked back a few steps.

"Well done, you did a good job," complimented William.

Donovan walked away looking ridiculously pleased.

Mighty Mouth who had watched the whole exchange strode over to William.

"Hey man, how did you hook him so quickly?"

"You snooze you lose," William laughed.

"I'll buy him from you," Mighty Mouth offered. "Name your price."

"No price," William said as he reached for his towel and hung it over the door.

Mighty Mouth didn't like that answer; he liked to be in control. William had hooked Donovan first and Mighty Mouth didn't like that arrogant fucker Mad Dog. He decided that he would drag Donovan away from William, irrespective of the cost.

William was walking down the path with Lenny and Angel, heading to to commissary.

"See that black mother-fucker up ahead in the line," asked William.

"Black, which one? There are hundreds of them or can't you tell the difference?" Angel quipped.

"Very funny asshole, the one who's getting head from the white punk there. That fucking pisses me off doing it in public. Anyway, when I get the chance I'm going to fuck him over."

"Just for getting head in public?" asked Lenny, adding, his voice betraying puzzlement, "That's a bit extreme even for you Mad Dog."

"Not just for that, but it's bad enough," William responded. He then explained about the interaction in the chow hall.

"Ok, now it makes sense," said Lenny. "We'll see what happens. Are you set up to take care of business."

"Always," William replied.

They had been waiting in line for two hours with the overbearing sun beating down contributing to the endless bitching that the line wasn't moving fast enough. A barrage of insults at everybody and nobody in particular occurred periodically. Occasional arguments broke out between inmates or passing officers.

"Put your shirt on," bellowed Lieutenant Hardy at a heavily tattooed member of the Aryan Brotherhood.

"Fuck you asshole, mind your own fucking business and fuck off," responded the particularly articulate gangster.

"What did you say to me, you fucking meat-head," demanded Hardy as he strode over towards Twiggy, so called because he was short and plump, the opposite of a twig. At this point in the interaction, everyone within earshot turned to see what transpired next.

"You heard what I said you fucking ignorant wife beating bitch."

Those choice of words served to incense Hardy more and he stepped up close to Twiggy, staring down at him breathing stale cigarette breath in his face.

"Say that again if you dare you fucking loser," raged Hardy.

"Back away from me before I beat the shit out of you, you fucking wife beating fucking bitch," responded Twiggy in a calm but hostile voice.

Lieutenant Hardy took a step backwards, not to comply with Twiggy's demand but to be in a less vulnerable position. Before anyone had chance to mutter an expletive Hardy had punched Twiggy with as much force as he could muster and caught him on the side of his temple. Twiggy, stunned for a moment, was overcome with rage and put his head down, barrelling into Hardy's midriff. The force of it sent them both sprawling onto the grass where a full, no holds barred fist fight commenced. The watching inmates screamed in support of Twiggy as the inmate and officer rolled on the ground raining blows on one another.

"Mad Dog, now is the time," urged Lenny.

The black inmate that William was intent confronting was skirting around the back of the crowd, standing on tiptoe to watch the fight. He wasn't aware of William, Lenny and Angel surrounding him.

One on each side of their target, Lenny and Angel pulled the guy away from the crowd and pushed him backwards towards William. He lost his footing and fell into William, making the next move easier for William. He held the guy's weight just long enough to deliver a stab in a strategic spot that reached his heart; the guy wouldn't be a further problem. William let the inmate fall and the three of them waited; seconds later the inmate was still, blood seeping from a single wound. William stood, wiped his blade on the dying man's shirt, turned to Lenny and Angel, suggesting that they rejoin the commissary line, now short since everyone was watching the fight.

From their distant position, the three protagonists heard then saw ten officers come running, each of them screaming for the inmates to step back. Everyone moved a couple of paces but continued to yell in support of Twiggy.

Twiggy was hauled off Hardy by three officers who threw him face down on the grass and wrenched his hands behind his back to cuff him. Two more officers helped Hardy up. He was covered in cuts and grazes as was Twiggy. The other officers stood in positions to hold back the inmates. Lieutenant Hardy was still raging and stormed over to where Twiggy was handcuffed face down on the grass. He rained a series of vicious kicks to his ribcage,catching him on the side of his head. The two officers who had restrained Twiggy leapt forward and pushed Hardy back to stop his renewed assault on the inmate.

"Calm down Lieutenant," said one of them as they kept a firm hold of his arms until they saw the rage dissipate.

"What the fuck was that about?" the officer asked.

"He's a fucking inmate isn't he!" stated Hardy as if that were reason enough and turned away, stomping off, leaving the officers glancing at each other, their face showing genuine concern over the incident.

"A loose fucking cannon, that's what he is," retorted the other officer.

William, Lenny and Angel ignored the drama as they sauntered back from commissary, arms laden with bags of food and goodies for the week. They were laughing and joking and only paid scant attention to what was going on but, as they opened the door to re-enter the prison building, they heard shouts about an inmate having been stabbed. They headed back to their pod, discussing the Burritos they would make for dinner.

Just another day in prison.

William had health issues and had been on medication for years. He'd contracted Hepatitis C from a dirty tattoo needle. Being a heroin addict and occasionally sharing needles hadn't helped either.

Over the last few months, William had noticed that one of his testicles was becoming enlarged. It didn't hurt, still seemed to function but was growing and changing in colour. After a year of seeing it enlarge, he decided it was time to see a doctor. From then on he mentioned it each time he visited the medical section for his Hep C meds. They took little interest, telling William that's wasn't why he was in medical, that he should put in a sick call. When he complied with their advice, it had taken up to ten days to be called to medical. On each occasion the doctor had told him that the swelling was nothing, that it happens sometimes. On one occasion a different doctor had told him that it was caused by an infection, probably from a mosquito bite, and issued him with a course of antibiotics. They had made no difference to the look or size of his ever growing testicle, which was now the size of a grapefruit and the colour of a plum.

He had been given a lay-in to go to medical to have blood tests for monitoring his Hep C. He was supposed to have them monthly but that didn't happen; since he'd been making a noise about his testicle problem the docs had been taking the blood. He had noticed during the last few weeks a shooting pain from his testicle up through his body whenever he moved too fast or tried to work out and it was causing him a modicum of concern. It wasn't the pain that bothered him, pain was something on which he thrived; he wanted to know what was going on in his body.

After Nurse Dracula had taken several phials of blood, he mentioned his enlarged and purple testicle to her. To her credit she called the doctor over to check him out, a bonus as a doctor actually there in person was a rare occurrence. Inmates normally saw their 'provider' via a monitor link.

What did you do?" asked Dr Chen.

"I don't know," said William. "It's been getting bigger over the past year."

"Why didn't you mention it before now," Dr Chen asked accusingly.

"I have tried to get it looked at every fucking time I come in here," William retorted. "No mother-fucker is interested."

"You need to jack off," declared the doctor.

William looked incredulous.

"I do not need to jack off. Why the fuck would I need to jack off?"

"You have water on your balls, you need to jack off then you'll be fine," insisted Dr Chen.

"What the fuck!" William proclaimed. "That is a load of bullshit. I jack off plenty and it doesn't make any difference to what is going on with my ball."

"Yes, you need to jack off every day and it will be ok," insisted the doctor. "I will check it next week, it should be ok by then."

"What about the colour of it, that's definitely not normal?"

"It's probably bruised."

"What the fuck are you talking about asshole. How would I bruise it?"

"I don't know, maybe fighting, maybe someone gave you head."

William looked at him contemptuously. "If someone gave me head, which they didn't, it would be the same as jacking off, so, by your crazy diagnosis, it would be fine. You're talking bullshit asshole."

"I told you what you have to do, so get out of here, I'm busy," the doctor said.

"Ok, you're the doctor but you are talking fucking bullshit. Are you even a real fucking doctor?" he asked as he went out of the door feeling contemptuous.

William took his prescribed medication for the Hep C. As Nurse Dracula watched him swallow it, an elderly white inmate came in the door.

"I'm not feeling good, my chest hurts."

"You look fine," declared the nurse giving an injection to another inmate. She gave him a once over. "Fuck off back to your house and stop wasting our time."

The elderly man looked distraught but didn't say anything as he turned back to the door to leave. William jumped ahead of him and held open the door for him as he didn't look like he had the strength to do it himself. William accompanied the senior down the hallway, recognising him vaguely, coming from the Trusty camp.

"You shouldn't let them treat you like that," said William. "Give those useless mother-fuckers hell. It's the only thing they understand."

The old man turned to look at William and smiled as he collapsed on the floor clutching his chest.

"Holy fuck," said William. "The mother-fuckers have killed him."

He looked along the hallway to see who was around.

"Huntley," he shouted. "Get your worthless ass over here, you've got a dead one. Medical have just killed him."

Huntley stopped in her tracks trying to make sense of what the crazy tattooed idiot had said. She thought she heard someone was dead, and indeed someone was lying on the floor. As she ran full pelt down the hall, the door to medical opened and Nurse Dracula emerged.

She surveyed the scene then shouted back through the door for someone to bring a gurney. Huntley stood at the scene puffing and panting; shapely she may have been but she was definitely out of shape.

"Oh my god, what am I supposed to do?" Huntley asked.

"Not my problem," replied William as he sauntered off back to his building.

15

"Where is my fucking shit?" Angel growled in the face of the officer he currently had by the neck against the wall of a cleaning cupboard.

"Fuck you asshole," croaked the Hispanic officer named Cruz. "Get your fucking hands off me."

"Where is my product you've been paid for," Angel queried again as he took his hand away from Cruz's neck, but remained close to the point where Cruz felt spots of spittle land on his face.

Cruz side-stepped him and said, wiping his face with the back of his hand, "I'll have it for you in a few days.".

"I should have had it last week mother-fucker, what is going on?"

"I'm having a bit of trouble with my supplier," Cruz admitted reluctantly.

"What sort of trouble?" Angel asked, now on edge.

"He hasn't been seen for a few days. I've been calling him but he doesn't answer his phone and he isn't hanging out where I usually see him," Cruz explained his face displaying the worry he felt inside.

He had become more concerned as the days went on. Cruz earned good money from Angel but it came with the understanding that there were to be no mistakes. Angel's reputation went before him, everyone knew of him; his renown was earned, he wasn't weak nor forgiving. On occasion Angel had overlooked a mistake but not often enough that anyone knew of it. He was ruthless, believed in harsh consequences for minor errors as a deterrent against carelessness, a bigger sin that led to big mistakes. Angel excelled at the enforcement side of the Cartel's business, using his vicious reputation to keep his people in line.

"You've two days. If you haven't brought it then you'll be dealt with," promised Angel in a quiet but menacing tone.

Two days later, Officer Cruz was on the unit on his way to see Angel with the product he was late supplying. Angel and Carlos' One and Two came out of the multi-purpose room that had been acting as church for services to be held. They were the last ones to leave as they had stayed behind to fetch the weekly supply from the priest who came in to perform the service for the Catholics. Carlos Two was the first to spot Cruz and, quick as a flash, grabbed his arm and pulled him inside the room, then shut the door leaving Carlos One outside as a guard.

"I have it for you," Cruz said after recovering from the surprise of being yanked from the hallway.

"About fucking time," barked Carlos Two and, without warning, punched Cruz in the centre of his soft belly then again, as he said, "Fuck-ups will not be tolerated."

Officer Cruz coughed and wheezed from the impact of the double punch.

"I got it in the end," said Cruz holding out his hand to Angel who took the proffered packages.

"The next supply is due in a few days. Don't fuck up again or you won't live long enough to regret it," warned Carlos Two giving Cruz a third punch to make his point clear.

Lieutenant Hardy chose that moment to open the door and enter the room and he pushed Carlos One inside in front of him. Hardy saw Carlos Two punch Officer Cruz. He didn't like Cruz, he considered him an inferior because he was Hispanic, but he wasn't going to ignore an officer being assaulted, even if it was by his own kind.

Carlos One, quick to react to the situation, pretended to stumble from the push and came to a stop in front of his boss. Angel surreptitiously handed him the packages.

"Well, well, well. What do we have going on here," he stated rather than asked. "Two inmates ganging up on an officer, even if he is a spineless, useless Mexican. Get up against the wall."

"What the fuck Hardy? I was on my way to work," Carlos Two complained. "The LT is waiting for me."

Hardy gave Carlos Two a brief glance as he said, "You'd better get to work then loser. Fuck off out of here."

Carlos One left the room without giving the others a second look. He closed the door behind him then headed straight for his section to hide the new delivery. Angel and Carlos Two did as they were told without saying a word. Officer Cruz stood hunched over, holding his stomach whilst glaring at Hardy. He hadn't appreciated or wanted the interruption. Awkward questions could be asked and he didn't have any acceptable answers.

"Well?" Hardy asked of no one in particular and no answer came. Hardy walked up to Carlos Two, told him to turn around with hands on the wall and Carlos Two complied. Hardy felt the desire to kick the inmate's feet wider apart then gave Carlos Two a thorough pat down. When he didn't find anything, he repeated the process with Angel.

"There is no way you mother-fuckers are clean. Cruz here is one of your suppliers?" he said throwing Cruz a distasteful look.

"Fuck you Hardy," retorted Cruz and stomped out of the room, averting his eyes from piercing stares heading his way. Hardy laughed.

"I want a cut," demanded Hardy, looking straight at Angel. Angel and Carlos Two both turned back around. "Either that or I am going to write you both up for assaulting an officer."

Angel gave a mocking laugh. "Do I look like I give a shit about a case, Hardy? You've got me fucked up if you think I care,"

"You sound just like that fucking loser Mad Dog," Hardy snarled in frustration. "Hang around with that mother-fucker a lot don't you?"

"What the fuck's it got to do with you?"

"Like I said, I want a cut of all the business you are doing."

"What business? I don't know what you're fucking talking about," Angel replied.

"Play dumb then."

Hardy took out his notepad and pen and wrote down the details so that he could issue them both with a disciplinary case later.

"I'm going to take down that fucking asshole Mad Dog. You'd better think about whether you want me to take you down too. I'll give you until the end of my shift to decide whether you want life to be easy or hard. Now fuck off before you make me mad."

16

William was walking back from the chow hall with Lenny and Angel. The young black female officer standing at the door watched the three of them walk towards her.

"Hey you, what are you stealing?"

All three of them looked at her in surprise.

"You." She pointed at William. "What do you have hidden in your pants?"

"What the fuck are you talking about? I haven't stolen anything or got anything down my pants," William replied.

"You have a big bulge in your pants."

"That's because I have the hots for you," William laughed.

"Fuck you asshole," she responded, "tell me what you have hidden or I'll write you up."

"Listen, you fucking useless bitch, I've told you I haven't stolen any food and I don't have anything down my pants."

"Come on Mad Dog, show her what you have down there," said Lenny, chuckling.

"Yeah Mad Dog, show her," said Angel.

"I'm giving you one last chance before I write you up mother-fucker. Return what you stole, now!"

"Fuck you bitch, write me up I don't give a fuck." William declared.

"That's it. Drop your fucking pants now," she ordered.

William grinned. "Ok."

William pulled his pants and shorts down exposing his whole lower body to everyone.

"Oh my fucking god," the young officer screamed.

William, Lenny and Angel stood laughing at the officer's reaction and William took a perverse pleasure from shocking her. She was horrified at the sight of his massively swollen purple testicle the size of a grapefruit.

"Mad Dog!"

All three of them looked over to hear who was shouting at William and watched as Officer Stead strode over.

"Pull your fucking pants up and fuck off back to your house. All you mother-fucker's, fuck off," he shouted, still fifty yards away.

"It's what I was trying to do boss. This bitch wouldn't let me," William said, labouring the words.

"Well I'm telling you. Fuck off."

Officer Stead turned on the young officer.

"Leave that fucking idiot alone. If you want trouble, he's going to give it to you."

Stead turned around and strode off the way he'd come.

17

When they returned to the day room, Old Man Lang was arguing with a younger black inmate, his cellie. Old Man Lang had his shower bag on the table in front of him, looking through it for the umpteenth time for something that should have been there but wasn't.

"Where is my soap, mother-fucker?"

"I don't know what you're talking about Old Man," said Dwayne shrugging his shoulders as he spoke.

"My soap. I know you fucking stole it. You are the only one who could have it. Give it back now," said Old Man Lang.

"I think you've gone gaga," said Dwayne, sighing heavily.

"You've two fucking choices: give my soap back or be sorry," growled Old Man Lang.

Dwayne looked at Old Man and laughed nervously as he said, "I d... don't have your fucking soap. Fuck off."

He saw the steely glint in the old man's eyes but now he couldn't back down.

"You saw me buy it at commissary yesterday. You knew I had a new bar of soap. You are the only one who had access to it in the house," Old Man Lang said, poking Dwayne in the chest, exaggerating each sentence.

"I haven't got your fucking soap. Fuck off and stop bothering me with that pussy-ass shit. You've lost the plot," said Dwayne, backing away and side-stepping Old Man Lang.

"If that's how you want to play it cellie, that's fine by me. You choose to be sorry and I'll oblige you with that.".

Dwayne chose to ignore Old Man Lang's mutterings as the ramblings of a senile old codger. Nevertheless, he was rattled, having heard stories about the old man, all gruesome. He didn't believe them, but it left him on edge. He mixed with some of his home-boys and tried to forget about the incident. Old Man Lang stood and stared at the back of Dwayne's head for a moment, deep in thought, then he strolled over to William's cell. He found

William stretched out on his bunk, reading a law book on how to structure his own appeal.

"Hey Mad Dog, I need a can of coke."

William sat and opened his locker. A few packets fell out and William removed more.

"Don't have coke, only root beer," William said, "How many do you want?"

"Just the one is enough thanks Mad Dog," he said and grinned.

William handed him the drink and glanced at his face. "Are you ok? What's going on?"

"Nothing's going on, everything is good. Don't worry about it Mad Dog," he paused before continuing "You know I've done thirty eight years in this system and I'm never going home. Things are changing Mad Dog and not for the better."

He finished abruptly, then walked back to his cell.

An hour later Old Man Lang exited his cell and Dwayne was still at the table. The old man walked up behind Dwayne, and lifted his arms up and over the front of Dwayne's face. The light was glinting off whatever was in Old Man's hands, sending flashes of light dancing around the walls. Old Man had a hand either side of Dwayne's neck and started moving them side to side in a sawing motion. A blood-curdling scream pierced the quiet of the day room as Dwayne felt the sheer metal of the diamond shaped, razor sharp serrated home-made saw slice through his neck. He grabbed at it, trying to pull it away from his neck but all he sensed was pain as his fingers were sliced open. Blood spurted across the table as his carotid artery was cut and his head was almost severed from his body. No one round the table moved as they looked on in shock and horror, blood splashing their white prison issue clothing. Old Man gave up when he met with greater resistance in his endeavour to cut the head clean off. He had achieved his aim; Dwayne would be sorry. That was the last bar of soap, or anything, he would be stealing. The murder had taken less than a minute and Old Man Lang let go of the former drinks can that had proven to be such a deadly weapon in his hands. He returned to his cell to wash off the blood and change his clothes. Then he dropped down onto his bunk and read a car magazine William had given him. He could hear the panic and disturbance going on in the day room and was sure that the laws would be coming for him imminently. He'd packed up his belongings before he had taken retaliatory action and was ready to move to twelve building segregation.

"What the fuck?" William said as he appeared at Old Man's door. Old Man looked up at him and smiled.

"I'll be back soon enough to continue our business arrangement, probably thirty days," he said calmly.

"What the fuck did he do?" William asked.

"Stole my new bar of soap, then denied it."

William laughed in admiration as he said, "Well you fixed his wagon, he won't be doing that again."

18

Candy came out of his cell. He had finished servicing the stream of guys that waited in line and they had all paid Mighty Mouth for their pleasure. Candy had been hooked by Mighty Mouth and his gang as he passed straight through the door of prison. New to the prison system, he'd only spent time in county jails before. He'd received a two year sentence for prostitution and drug possession and had been assessed by the judge, who told him that he clearly had no desire to turn his life around.

As with many inmates caught up in the system, Candy's path to incarceration had been predictable: father beat him for being different, mother who couldn't protect him for fear of being beaten herself, thrown out to fend for himself on the streets as a teenager and falling prey to older, more street smart predators. He'd stolen ladies clothes from a department store and touted his trade on street corners dressed as a female hoping to pick up clients who would appreciate what he was offering. Most days he managed to earn enough to feed himself and his drug habit. Speed was his drug of choice, it perked him up and gave him a confidence to sell himself, something he wouldn't have had without the drug. When business was slow he'd spend nights with a cup of coffee in fast food restaurants or twenty four hour supermarkets. Occasionally, during the day, he'd go into a good hotel and sleep curled up in one of the over-sized armchairs that were a mainstay of the better class of establishment. He would also wash and clean in the public toilets. If he was lucky he would wangle his way into the hotel's gym, usually by waiting for someone to open the door. That way he could also utilise the showers and complimentary toiletries that were offered.

Candy, whose real name was Brian. would often contemplate on how his life had become so desperate. Before being thrown out onto the street, he had dreamed of going to university and pursuing a career in law. He had known from a very young age that the chances of that happening were zilch, without a miracle. He had occupied his time as a teenager in the local library reading law books, trying to make sense of the complex legalese. His dreams had not diminished but were certainly dimmed by his current predicament.

When Candy entered the prison he had been taken to medical for the routine health check and been spotted by Mighty Mouth.

Mighty Mouth was a seasoned convict who had arrived at prison in his late twenties. He'd served eighteen years of a forty year sentence for kidnapping and torturing young homeless boys, grooming them and forcing them into prostitution, as gay boys and she-males. He had made a lucrative living from the misery and deprivation of the boys and, in the process, had built up a huge exclusive client list.

He was a huge black man who had no remorse for his crimes and no qualms about continuing his reign of terror behind bars, seeing it as an extension to his business in the free world. There were no shortage of youngsters in prison to subjugate, just a matter of how to snare and reel them in.

William had been keeping a close eye on Mighty Mouth and his activities and had ended up on the wrong side of Mighty Mouth right through the door. This didn't concern William but it was prudent to keep a close eye on Mighty Mouth and his activities because of the animosity. His altercation as William was released from seg had been a belittling moment for Mighty Mouth; it wouldn't be forgotten or forgiven, at some point there would be retaliation.

William had taken notice of Mighty Mouth's activities with the she-males. He seemed to control six that William had identified, two being on their section. Mighty Mouth treated his punks atrociously, refusing to take care and protecting them as was his duty, ensuring that they would bend over whenever was required. He allowed them to be abused, even beaten up, by his clients. William didn't like that and, to his way of thinking, it was counter-productive and would bring Karma down on him. Blacks were not known for this way of thinking and Mighty Mouth, in particular, took pleasure in treating them as badly as possible, abuse at it's finest.

William had identified two she-males he was going to take from Mighty Mouth: Candy and his friend Sparkle. Both were attractive, feminine looking types with massive profit margins. Sparkle was a confident, outgoing and bubbly type, not subject to the abuses that Candy endured. Sparkle tried to teach Candy how to be more assertive as a survival technique whilst in the system. They were living on the same pod as William so it was easy for him to watch their activities, see how many guys they were servicing each day.

William watched Mighty Mouth insult and berate Candy whenever he griped about the abusive treatment meted out. Mighty Mouth bellowed, telling him that he should be grateful that he was being protected. How much worse did he think it would be if he Mighty Mouth wasn't his guardian?.

Candy didn't think it could be worse without Mighty Mouth's so called protection, but was too scared to say anything. He looked around the day room after receiving another cruel tongue-lashing and locked eyes with William. William stared straight at him but there was nothing to be read on his face. Candy dropped his eyes, retreating to his cell, wondering about ways to end his misery.

Mighty Mouth was unhappy and Mad Dog aggravated his temper. Everywhere he looked, Mad Dog was there, everywhere he went, Mad Dog was being discussed. Why? He didn't know. It wasn't like the guy was anyone special, just some worthless punk who talked big and was always surrounded by a crowd. Not just Peckerwoods either (white guys who would fight), although there were plenty of them, and there were a couple of blacks from the hood who would hang out with him occasionally, plus that Mexican, Angel.

He had heard about Angel and his family. They were the big leagues; he didn't want to find himself on the wrong side of that cartel. There were hundreds of their members just in this unit, no telling how many across the whole system and they were brutal when crossed. That wasn't the business Mighty Mouth was in and he didn't want to attract unnecessary attention from the Mexicans. As it was, they made it clear that his business methods didn't pass the muster, as far as they were concerned.

Why was some loud-mouth arrogant mother-fucker like Mad Dog so tight with Angel? That, he couldn't understand.

19

Wilbur was an insignificant looking thirty year old black man, serving a six year sentence for shoplifting. He had been taking psych medications for a few years, since he'd been gang raped by seven members of a black gang on a different unit. Although the majority of sex offenders encountered no issues when incarcerated, Wilbur had attracted attention with his strange and socially incompatible ways. He would go up to someone, or a group of men, and place himself in the middle of the conversation and approach random inmates, asking for food or coffee. He would listen to conversations and give advice and opinions, usually not wanted and none of these behaviours went down well. It was difficult to figure out whether Wilbur was trying to create a situation or if he had an underdeveloped sense of self preservation. Either way, his actions were appreciated by no one and most guys avoided him, though some would threaten him and he'd taken several beatings for his unorthodox behaviour.

One day, after taking a shower, he returned to his cell and seven black guys had cornered him. He hadn't thought anything of it at first until he'd been pushed up against the wall and a large hand clamped over his mouth; then he realised he was in trouble. By then he couldn't shout, scream or make any type of sound except a low growl in his throat, which no one outside of his seven attackers heard. Someone stuffed his sock in his mouth and was aware of thinking to himself thank goodness my socks are clean. It didn't help as the sensation of choking and gagging overwhelmed him as the sock was forced into his mouth. Tears of fear and humiliation trickled down his face. Two guys, either side of him, held his arms, forcing them up his back so that he couldn't move, except to bend forward to relieve the pain from being forced into an unnatural position. Whilst he was still focussing on minimising the agonising suffering, he felt hands on his hips and a hard forceful thrust from behind. He tried to scream from the shock and the pain and couldn't believe what was happening to him. The thrusting was so forceful that he felt like he was being cut in two; he panicked. Unable to breathe, gagging from the sock filling his whole mouth, he tried to spit it out but there was too much material and it was thick and bulky. As he managed to spit some out, it was pushed back. Finally, the ordeal finished and he started to cry, from pain, shock and humiliation.

Why had this happened to him? Before he could think any further, he felt it happen again but, this time, not for as long, but it was more violent. Seven times in total it reoccurred, until each of the guys had taken their turn. After they had finished, they let him go and walked from his cell laughing but they hadn't seen the young Mexican guy, Abram walking to the shower block. He had glanced into Wilbur's cell; it wasn't usual to see multiple guys in his house. He saw what happened and witnessed the shock on Wilbur's face as he watched through a small gap in the door.

As Abram walked back to his cell he watched as the seven assailants leave and noted their identities.

Wilbur remained where he was for a long time after the attack. He was bleeding, seeing the blood running down his, leg though not registering it. In shock, he could think of nothing.

"What the fuck's wrong with him?" asked Carlos, a short squat young Mexican with huge muscles threatening to rip open his shirt sleeves. One of Angel's trusted men, albeit currently on a different unit, he was also Wilbur's cellie but Carlos spoke to him little, except what was necessary to co-habit together in an twelve by eight feet space.

"I don't know, he's not saying anything," answered Alfonso, Carlos' elderly neighbour and work partner in the laundry. "I don't think he even knows we're here. He looks totally out of it but he's blood running down him. Go and call the law over, let him deal with him."

"What are we supposed to tell the law. It's not like they care anyway. Maybe I should talk to him?" said Carlos.

Abram had gone back to his cell, took out his writing paper and pencil and written a note about what he'd witnessed. He gave specific details, identifying the perpetrators with their cell and bunk numbers. He then went to chow and gave the note to a Captain who was supervising the chow hall.

Half an hour later all hell let loose in the pod and a dozen ninja turtles, suited and booted, stormed in, each screaming at everyone to immediately get down on the floor. The inmates not already in their cells dropped to the floor wondering what was going on. Captain Gonzalez, who had accompanied the ninja turtles, strode over to the showers and found Wilbur, naked and bloodied curled up in the corner of his cell. He hadn't moved and was unresponsive to whatever the Captain said, even as he shouted at Wilbur. The only reaction was when tears rolled silently down Wilbur's cheeks. Gonzalez retired to the desk where a duty officer was seated, looking bemused, wondering why the day room was full of the Swat team. It struck him as being rather extreme.

"Call medical and bring a wheelchair immediately," instructed Gonzalez.

He then turned to the day-room and called out cell and bunk numbers. After shouting each number, he waited for an offender to step forward. When the second one had been called, the seven knew what it was about and stood, resolutely mute.

Two nurses, one male, one female turned up with a wheelchair and blanket. Gonzalez went with the female and the desk officer to deal with Wilbur, who hadn't moved since Gonzalez checked him earlier. The medical team helped him into the wheelchair, covered him with the blanket and the nurse then took him off to the medical wing.

Each perpetrator was handcuffed behind his back and escorted by two ninja turtles, holding tightly to each of his arms. Shady, the self appointed leader of the gang was unhappy with the developments. As he was having his hands wrenched behind his back, he swivelled round and head-butted one of the ninjas. The ninjas were wearing helmets with clear Plexi-glas to protect their face so the aggression was futile. In response, two appointed ninjas threw him to the ground and one of them placed his booted foot across the back of the inmate's shoulders as the other handcuffed him unnecessarily roughly. All seven were taken to twelve building and charged with statutory rape. They would serve a minimum twelve month stint in segregation, plus the prospect of facing free-world charges. Gang officers first interviewed and then moved Wilbur to another unit for his own protection; he spoke little, still traumatised by the assault.

20

After his unit transfer, Wilbur spent two and a half years on the psych building, being dosed up daily to help him deal with his PTSD and depression from his ordeal. They didn't help; simply dulled his senses, made him sleep a lot and he became sluggish. No counselling was on offer for his issues, so he was unable to put his horrific ordeal behind him. It played havoc with his mind and frequently his thoughts drifted between suicide, revenge, and murder. So far these were only thoughts, but one day...

Wilbur's whole personality had altered, no longer socialising with anyone, staying in his cell for as much time as he could and withdrawing into himself. He had taken to drawing but his pictures were dark and disturbing in content. They were kept in an ever growing folder and he would take them out daily to inspect, taking inspiration from some for his next work. Wilbur would stand at his door and watch, everyone and everything. Both inmates and officers found Wilbur unnerving and tried to avoid him, which was easy to do since Wilbur interacted with no one, barely speaking, even when essential. Self imposed extreme social isolation only served to make his condition deteriorate.

Wilbur had been moved into a general population building. It was clear that he didn't belong there with his psychological issues but, with an absence of unruly and psychotic behaviours of others, plus the extreme shortage of beds in the psych building, he was moved out. He had been on the new pod for a few weeks, spooking many of the inhabitants. Others had been quietly studying him and Wilbur knew this, because he was watching them, watching him.

There was one tiny ray of light for Wilbur from his move. The father of his childhood friend was here, Mighty Mouth, who had looked out for him as a child as Wilbur had spent most of his time at Mighty Mouth's house. The big man took Wilbur under his wing, barely recognising the person that Wilbur had become. Wilbur confided in Mighty Mouth who issued a 'hit' on the seven who had raped Wilbur. They were now in different units, but this didn't matter to Mighty Mouth, his reach went far and wide. The irony that he was responsible for inflicting the same horrors on other vulnerable youngsters was lost on him.

Wilbur slowly became more unstable, inhabiting the general population, the absence of regular medication being the main culprit. General population contrasted starkly to the calm of the psych building and Wilbur was finding it difficult to cope with the much faster pace of life. It was a constant battle for Wilbur to receive his medication as some of his medications were KOP (keep on person), whilst others he had to fetch from pill window. Many of the officers didn't care about inmate's medications, so didn't bother to call them to take for their meds. Others hated all inmates and would make life difficult for them during the eight hours they worked before going home. Others were 'jobsworths', officers who made life difficult for inmates, refusing or unable to be flexible as situations required. A few officers did care or, at best were professional, ensuring inmates did what was required of them and received what they needed. These were the officers who understood that, being fair with the inmates, made for a calmer, easier and safer life for everyone. Officers with a conscience, a rare beast.

"Rack up, Rack up, Rack up," shouted the desk officer ; at first no one took any notice and inmates continued to talk on the phone, take showers, or play cards.

"Rack up *now*," the officer screamed.

"What the fuck?" exclaimed several inmates. "What the fuck for?"

"Rack up you mother-fuckers," the officer screamed again.

"Why the fuck do we have to rack up?" demanded Lenny.

"Short of staff," responded the officer, screaming again, "Rack up now."

Everyone grumbled, complained and vilified the administration while slowly gathering their items together to take back in their houses. There was no choice; failure to comply came with severe repercussions.

Being racked up at weekends was becoming tedious and causing tension in the unit. It had been happening for weeks and the atmosphere throughout the unit was palpably hostile. If more weekend staff weren't found soon, there was going to be a riot.

"Let me go to pill window," said Wilbur.

"Too late," said the desk officer overseeing the pod. "I already called pill window a while ago. Now rack up and shut the fuck up."

"I never heard you, let me out the door, I need to get my meds," said Wilbur.

"Hey bitch, it's your job to make sure he goes to pill window. You never called him, so let him go before you regret it," interjected Mighty Mouth.

"Rack up now or you'll be sorry," snarled the officer.

"I need my meds! Let me get my meds! I need them now! Open the fucking door!"

"Fuck off and........."

The officer stopped speaking abruptly and didn't see or feel the blow to the face as Wilbur head-butted him. He dropped like a stone to the floor unaware of what had happened.

The officer in the picket had been snoozing and saw nothing of what was happening but he woke abruptly as, out of nowhere, fighting started, en-masse. This situation provided men with the opportunity to settle scores and they wasted little time.

21

William was on his bunk with his arms propping up his head. He was laughing and joking with Lenny, Angel, and Rat, recently arrived on the unit with a twenty five year sentence for gun running. The subject of their hilarity were the jobs they'd pulled in the past but their fun was interrupted when they heard the riot kick off.

They reminisced about stealing ATM machines, the lengths they went to to make sure they succeeded and how Lenny would steal cars to order, and find ones to use for their criminal activities to discard after the job was complete.

Drugs figured too, to whom they'd been and how. Angel told the guys about William's non-existent sense of direction when driving across country delivering large volumes of drugs for the Cartel, how he needed written directions. Angel told of how he'd been ordered by his father to make sure that William delivered exclusively for the cartel; he'd gone into a rage when informed that William had refused, continuing to deliver for the competition too.

They talked flippantly of murders they had committed or knew had happened and were in their element, discussing their lifestyle and old times, the only lifestyle they'd known. To them, this was normality.

William asked Rat about his family, parents Jeannie and Peter who had always treated William like a son, even though they had four of their own, each a wildcat. Rat told of how he had taken the rap for his dad Pete, who had been delivering a cargo of firearms on his behalf. Pete had been stopped for an inspection and the extra cargo had been found. Rat's older brothers, Mark and Richie were both married with families, Mark happily, with two children, and Richie with three children and a wife who left him and her children for another man. Both Mark and Richie joined their father in the trucking business, a lucrative and flexible industry, allowing them to take care of their families, plus Ginger's children too. Rat and William reminisced, telling stories about Rat's youngest brother and William's former best friend. He'd been killed by Lieutenant Clark during a riot; Clark had been permanently dealt with.

Angel looked thoughtful for a while then asked a few questions about Lieutenant Clark.

"That explains a lot," said Angel mysteriously, pausing. The others looked at him for clarification.

"You know Clark and Hardy are, or were half brothers," he said.

William was momentarily struck dumb until he said, "Are you fucking sure?"

"Yep, definitely. My granddad knew the mother, who tell him that the brothers had a sadistic streak," said Angel.

"No shit. That's the understatement of the year. It also explains why that mother-fucker Hardy hates me like he does. Probably not a good idea to let him know that we know his family history," said William, a grin spreading across his face.

Angel looked over to where the explosion of noise came from.

"Hey, come and see this. Wilbur has really gone crazy."

The other three jumped up to take a look. William and Rat glanced around at the picket and saw the officer, with his feet up on the desk, asleep.

"Let's just watch to see how this plays out," said Angel and the others agreed. It made a change for them not to be in the thick of the action.

Wilbur was uncontrollable and Mighty Mouth, with one of his minions, were trying to drag Wilbur away from the unconscious officer, without success. Wilbur finally snapped,stomping and kicking with a fury that made him feel invincible. He was releasing his pent up hatred, anger and pain; there was no stopping him until he was free from the shackles of his psychosis. When Wilbur's legs tired of kicking and stomping the now obliterated head, he turned to jumping on the torso, determined to do as much damage to it as had been done to him.

The officer in the picket opened his eyes and took a lazy look around. He spotted William, Lenny, Angel and Rat stood in the doorway of a cell on one row. He clocked Wilbur jumping up and down on someone, but couldn't make out who it was. Ninety percent of the inmates in the day room were fighting, he figured as the officer heard a blood-curdling scream.

He didn't immediately process what was going on in E pod but, when he did, leapt out of his chair and pushed the emergency button, which set off a screeching clang, reminiscent of a fire alarm. He punched the button on the tannoy and screamed at the fighting inmates, telling them to lie down on the floor. This fell on deaf ears do he repeated the command several times with increasing volume.

He opened the window and shrieked his command again, to no avail as none of the inmates took any notice. This infuriated the officer who hated inmates; they had no morals nor discipline, something valued discipline above everything else.

He made another attempt. Nothing, so he slammed shut the window just in time to open the door to the pod for a dozen officers, including suited and booted ninjas, to storm in to take control. The officer stood at the window to watch the proceedings unfold.

"Get down on the ground." shouted several of the crack team at once.

As soon as Mighty Mouth saw that the officer attacked by Wilbur was dead, he grabbed Wilbur, dragging him round to the stairs.

"Get up to your cell now," he said.

Wilbur looked at Mighty Mouth with a dazed expression but did as he was told, taking the stairs two at a time up to three row. He didn't enter his cell though, instead stood at the half wall looking down at what was going on, still dazed, not understanding what was going on below. Wilbur had no recollection of what he had just done.

Whilst several of the officers continued to shout instructions at the inmates, the ninja turtles went around the room securing inmates that showed any signs of being involved in the rioting. Those wise to the system had retired to their cells or sat against the wall.

"What the fuck…" said Officer Stead as he stepped in a thick pool of blood.

"Who the fuck is that?" he asked of nobody in particular.

Shocked at what he was seeing, even after the years he had worked in the prison system; this was the worst he'd witnessed. Officer Stead couldn't bring himself to look at the body, one with hardly a recognisable head. He averted his eyes, stared up to the picket and told the officer to open his window.

"Did you see who did this?"

The picket officer looked around the day room, along each row until he spotted Wilbur. "Him. Up on three row. I saw him kicking and stomping, but couldn't tell who it was on the receiving end."

"Get medical over here now," said Officer Stead.

Stead strode across to the day room and placed himself at the bottom of the stairs as he yelled, "Wilbur, get your sorry ass down here before I send SWAT up to get you."

Wilbur looked at him and shook his head as three of the SWAT team joined Officer Stead, ready to retrieve Wilbur at Stead's command.

"Get your fucking worthless ass down here, you fucking deranged psycho," said Lieutenant Hardy, his voice harsh, "I'll show you what happens to fucking psychos who kill officers. Get your bitch-ass down here now."

Everyone in the pod was silent as they watched the inevitable for there was no doubt that Wilbur would be read the riot act. He was carted away by the ninjas, clear that it was not going to be an easy ride for him.

William, Lenny, Rat and Angel had remained in the doorway of William's cell throughout the whole drama and had a prime view of Wilbur and the unfolding events.

"Do you think he'll give up easily?" Rat asked.

"No way," said Lenny.

"I don't know, " interjected Angel, "he looks like little boy lost."

"Nah," said William. "He's going to take a dive."

"Fuck off, no way," said Lenny. "I'll bet a coke and a packet of chocolate chip cookies on it."

"You're on," said William, cementing their bets, then turning back to watch the scene.

The three ninjas ran up the first set of stairs to two row.

"Don't come near me, stay where you are." Wilbur shouted in panic for he knew what would happen to him if the ninjas reached him. He'd be restrained, dragged away and beaten before reaching the infirmary. The ninjas were legendary and the treatment they dished out at their pleasure was common knowledge.

William knew it only too well; he was frequently at the mercy of the ninja turtles' unauthorised treatment and had racked up dozens of assaults on officers whilst restrained. Those who knew William were wary of him, because he accepted that retaliation beatings were part and parcel of prison life. For William, they were no deterrent and he would laugh about it, even joke with the ninjas. They mocked him about the number of times they'd 'accidentally' tripped him on the way to medical when William was checked over; they were doing their job was William's subjective view, and he wasn't going to make it easy for them. Everyone knew that the ninja's would reap their revenge on those who assaulted one of their own. It was part of 'the game'.

Officer Stead signalled to the SWAT team to remain put as Wilbur climbed onto the railings and perched precariously on top.

"What are you planning on doing there, Psycho?" said Lieutenant Hardy. "Intending to jump?"

"Wilbur, don't do anything stupid, get down and let's talk about what happened here," said Officer Stead as he gave Hardy a look that said 'shut the fuck up asshole'. Hardy laughed and continued his taunting.

"You haven't got the fucking nerve Psycho. You're too spineless to jump."

Wilbur started to panic, unsure why they were messing with him. Why couldn't they all just leave him alone?

"Take it easy, Wilbur," said Mighty Mouth from down below. "Don't let that fucking asshole get to you."

A smile drifted across Lieutenant Hardy face and he gave a deep chortle.

"You're useless aren't you Psycho?"

"Shut the fuck up, you idiot," hissed Officer Stead at Hardy.

"It's just a bit of fun, Stead, chill out. Isn't that right Psycho? We're just having a bit of fun."

The ninjas on the stairs shuffled around.

"Go and get the fucker," instructed Lieutenant Hardy to the ninjas.

"Don't fucking move," countered Officer Stead. The ninjas glared at him in frustration but didn't move.

"Come on down Psycho. One way or the other, I don't care. You know you're headed for seg."

"You know we're coming for you Psycho, make it easy on yourself and us," chimed in one of the ninjas on the stairs, moving up a step and pulling a pair of handcuffs from his belt. He clanked them together suggestively and Wilbur glanced at him, then looked back down at Hardy.

"I'll jump," Wilbur said, his voice an octave higher.

"Go ahead, it's not like anyone cares. Do yourself and everyone a favour and jump but make sure you do a proper job of it. If you have to be scraped off the concrete, at least it will add some colour to the floor," Hardy said, then adding, "Nobody will miss you. What is the point of you Psycho? Your worthless pitiful life isn't worth living."

Wilbur scanned around the day room, tears rolling down his cheeks. Everything Hardy said was true, he knew that; he was worthless, pathetic and spineless. He had just taken it, not fought back when he was horrifically abused. What was the point? This was no kind of life.

"Come on Psycho. Jump. I don't have all day. I want to go to lunch," said Lieutenant Hardy.

Whilst Lieutenant Hardy was coaxing Wilbur, the ninjas waiting impatiently on two row gave each other an imperceptible nod and exploded into action, taking the stairs to three row two and three at a time. Wilbur turned to see what they were doing as his face took on a grimace before he dove, head first, off the railings.

A burst of cheering erupted from the day room. Most inmates had seen suicides before, be it a hanging, an overdose or taking a dive like Wilbur had just done. Some inmates loved the drama involved in a suicide and others thought it the best way out of a never-ending saga of the mundane, often violent environment that was prison life. What achieved maximum approval was that it made a mess for the officers with reports, investigations, and the inevitable cleaning up.

Wilbur hit the concrete head first, forcing Lieutenant Hardy to jump back. Nearby tables, attached stools, floor and wall were immediately splattered with blood and brain matter.

"About fucking time," said Hardy looking down at his brain spattered clothes with distaste. "I'll leave you to clean up the mess Stead."

There was good reason why Hardy was hated by the inmates and other officers; he represented everything that was wrong with the system.

"Told you," said William, "Pay up losers."

Mighty Mouth was unhappy about what had happened to Wilbur, laying the blame entirely at Hardy's door. What made him madder was that Hardy was a regular client of his. The officer hadn't paid for services. Instead, he was supposed to protect Wilbur from the worst that prison would throw at him as a form of payment. He'd supplied Candy to service Hardy, who liked to be rough and abusive. Candy didn't dare complain; the one time he had plucked up the courage to bellyache, Mighty Mouth had beaten him to within an inch of his life. Mighty Mouth would approach Hardy; he didn't take kindly to being shafted.

The resulting investigation into the events surrounding the riot was the usual whitewash with the officers exonerated and the provocative behaviour of Lieutenant Hardy ignored. The fault was laid squarely on Wilbur who had no one in the free world to fight for him. It was easy for the Department of Corrections to close the book. Lieutenant Hardy had tried to have Officer Stead fired but failed on the grounds that the video evidence showed that Stead followed procedure. Case closed.

22

Mighty Mouth was still smarting about Wilbur. Besides looking after him, Mighty Mouth entrusted his money for safe-keeping to Wilbur. He knew no-one went near Wilbur. He'd barely left his cell so was reliable for stashing cash and keeping it safe for him. Mighty Mouth had shown Wilbur how to hide the money, a risk free strategy, or so Mighty Mouth thought, as Wilbur received only a cursory search of his cell, even when the law was searching for contraband.

Mighty Mouth had hundreds of dollars stashed in the wall behind the toilet. The problem was, now that someone else had moved into the cell, was how to retrieve it. He had offered to pack up Wilbur's sparse belongings, but Officer Stead had done it himself, giving the paintings to Mighty Mouth as Wilbur had no family; it seemed a shame to throw them away.

Mighty Mouth took the paintings, unsure what he would do with them. Inmates had limited storage space so he decided to send them home to his son. He was more concerned with retrieving his money before the new tenant discovered it.

William had been keeping a close watch on the interactions between Mighty Mouth and Wilbur and had seen Mighty Mouth slip money to Wilbur in his doorway, and stand guard whilst Wilbur hid it. At these times, William would take a walk up to three row to visit Angel and Lenny and stroll past Wilbur's door on the way. It was clear to William, from Wilbur's stance where he was storing the cash. Mighty Mouth would snarl at William, telling him to mind his own business as William stopped and tried to look in the cell. William would ignore Mighty Mouse and walk on with a grin on his face. His reason for wandering by was two fold: firstly, to check the hiding place hadn't changed and, secondly, to annoy Mighty Mouth. Mighty Mouth became more nervous each time William passed by.

As luck would have it for William, extremely bad luck for Mighty Mouth, an acquaintance of William's moved into the cell. Teacher was an average looking black man, neither big nor small. He had earned his nickname as a teenager when he enraged his gangster family by telling them that he was not going to join the 'family business'. He declared that he was aiming for university and then become a teacher. During his teenage years he had helped others with school-work when they were struggling. Teacher was naturally academic,deciding at a young age that he didn't want to live the life of his family, like drug-taking, criminal activity, jumping to attention whenever the Cartel wanted anything doing and the police constantly at the door. Throughout his teenage years he had been derided by the police and others in authority, tarred with the same brush as the rest of his family. He knew his time to leave would come; in the meantime he studied, learned and studied more.

His younger brother and his cousin had taken particular offence at his 'betrayal' of the family,spending months deciding how they could cause trouble for Teacher. They were going to ruin him, ensure that he had no option other than to rely on his criminal family. Teacher had been cajoled into going to dinner with the family. He'd been in sporadic contact with his mother, a strained affair; she made out that every bad thing that befell the family was on his head.

Teacher left the dinner early after accusations and blame were thrown his way again but he didn't get involved in the debate. Instead, he would sigh, stand up and then leave. That night, he retrieved his coat and walked out of the door and, as he walked to his car, two cop cars screeched to a halt, sirens blaring. A pair of cops shoved him to the ground, kicked him over onto his front and yanked his hands behind his back to cuff him. Then, he was pulled up to a standing position, patted down and searched as he looked on helplessly as the cops pulled small packages from both of his coat pockets. Due process was abandoned and Teacher was given a ten year sentence for possession and intent to distribute Cocaine and Heroin.

Teacher had been stoic, believing his sentence would be overturned on appeal, but, of course it hadn't.

Teacher had fallen lucky with his first cellie. William knew about Teacher through his dealings with the cartels as word had spread like wildfire on the streets. William had taken teacher under his wing, taught him the ropes, and how to endure. Teacher's survival technique differed from William's; they were different temperaments but William wanted Teacher to have no issues when they were no longer cellies.

Reputations are everything in prison, be it good or bad, and each had it's uses. Teacher wasn't a fighter so William reckoned that it was pointless teaching him how to take a fight to someone. It needed to be Teacher's own skill-set that would earn him safety. William identified those inmates who wanted to improve themselves to give them a chance on the outside. Teacher taught them how to read and write, fill out job applications, present themselves for interviews and handle themselves in different social settings. He then began to help with researching and writing appeals. This improved his credibility, coupled with the fact that everyone knew that he was protected by William. He was highly prized and William had shown Teacher how to make a healthy income from helping others. At first Teacher was reluctant at making money; he liked helping others, but William explained that everything in prison had a price tag. Give things away and you make yourself a target William instructed, and, over time, Teacher understood and began to make a healthy income.

Teacher stood in his door looking out over the day room to watch what has happening. Mighty Mouth looked up and spotted him. He made a beeline for the new guy and said, 'Hey man, is this your cell?'

"Just moved in not half an hour ago," replied Teacher.

"What's your name?"

"I'm known as Teacher."

"Teacher? Where have I heard that name before?" Mighty Mouth said as a light bulb turned on in his brain. "That's right, I know your family. We did a some business together a few years ago.'

If he thought this would impress Teacher, it hadn't and Mighty Mouth failed to see Teacher's reaction which was utter distaste for the loser standing in front of him.

"Hey, do you want to join our spread later? Me and some of the boys always cook together and share food."

"No thanks, I'm good. I like to keep myself to myself." Teacher knew that saying this wouldn't deter Mighty Mouth or others, but it was a start in re-establishing himself at a new unit.

Mighty Mouth frowned at the rebuff but, before he could comment, there was a commotion at the door. Both men turned to look.

"Mad Dog, how many times have I told you to stop giving food away to your homies!"

"Every fucking day Stead, I'm getting bored of hearing it."

"Well stop giving all the food away you fucking lunatic."

William grinned at Officer Stead and said, "Whatever you say Boss. See you tomorrow."

William scanned the day room, a simple precaution to see what he was walking into. Everything was calm...ish with the blacks screaming at some football game on the television. The whites were trying to watch a movie on the other television but could hear nothing for the racket coming from the opposite side. The Hispanics were out on the concrete recreation yard doing their daily extended workout in the blazing sun.

Just another day in prison, thought William.

"Hey Mad Dog."

William looked up to see from where the unfamiliar voice was coming. He saw the bulk of Mighty Mouth, then spotted the much smaller black man beside him.

"Hey Teacher, what are you doing here? Did you run out of victims at your last unit?" William said, breaking into a laugh.

Mighty Mouth was fuming.

What is it with that fucking Mad Dog that he ruins everything I am doing.

His interest was piqued by William's 'victims' comment.

William bounded up the stairs, stopped at the top, then bent over with a look of pain on his face.

"Are you ok Mad Dog?" Teacher said, with a look of concern on his face.

The moment passed and William stood upright. "I'm fine, just got a grapefruit for a ball and it gives me trouble now and again."

William saw Teacher wince and told him that it was nothing, and to forget it.

"Hey Mighty Mouth, you'd better not be harassing my boy here. We go back a long way."

Mighty Mouth looked straight at Teacher and snarled at him As he said, "So you're still a race traitor, hanging out with the white boys. You'd better watch your back."

"Bring it on, if you dare," said William. He knew that a confrontation with Mighty Mouth was inevitable; sooner rather than later suited William, on his terms with William controlling the situation. Mighty Mouth's size was irrelevant to William who had built his reputation on challenging the biggest guy on the block.

"Oh yeah," said Mighty Mouth, moving forward, his face close to William's. Bad move. William was ready and gave Mighty Mouth a right hook that would have downed most people. Mighty Mouth staggered from the force of the punch and William took full advantage. Queensbury rules played no part in William's fights; he played dirty, no holding back. William followed through with a knee to the face and a kick to the midriff as Mighty Mouth dropped to the floor, blood spewing all over the place. Not letting up, William followed through with a barrage of kicks and stomps to Mighty Mouth's head. He was out of it, knocked out as William finished him off with a few stomps to his hands. With a final kick to the side of the head, William strolled into Teacher's cell to wash himself off.

Teacher followed him, now hardened to prison life, and said "You haven't changed at all Mad Dog."

"Why would I change, I'm good with who I am."

William dropped down to his knees and started fiddling with the grill behind the toilet. 'Watch the door.'

"What are you doing?" Teacher said.

"Giving you a new unit starting fund," replied William. "You know the rules, don't tell anyone."

Teacher nodded as William scrabbled around behind the toilet. He knew that William had found what he was seeking when William's face displayed a huge smile.

He replaced the grill then sat on Teacher's bunk. Taking a bundle of cash from a plastic bag, he started counting it: two thousand seven hundred dollars. Damn. Mighty Mouth must have been confident that no one would find his money. That was a lot to keep around and must have delivering it to his mule to take to the free world bank. Too bad, it was William's now.

"Mad Dog, the law is coming up the steps," said Teacher, lowering his voice.

"Come and join me, we're just talking," said William as he stood up and hid the pile of money, safely back in the plastic bag, behind his huge discoloured testicle.

As an afterthought, he took two fifty dollar bills, ducked out of the door and slipped the money into Mighty Mouth's shirt pocket.

"Don't say I'm not generous," he said to the unresponsive Mighty Mouth. "I own those girls now."

The laws would be certain to find the money on his person. Mighty Mouth was heading for seg and, when he found out about the hundred dollars in his pocket, he'd understand that William had found his stash. William smiled to himself, a perverse pleasure decorating that thought.

"It's good to see you Teach."

When the officers reached three row, they saw Mighty Mouth unresponsive on the floor. One bent down to check on him whilst the other readied a can of pepper spray, should it be needed. The officer nudged Mighty Mouth with the toe of his boot. The only response was a groan so the officer used his foot to turn Mighty Mouth over. As he did, he spotted an unusual flash of green in the inmate's shirt pocket. He pulled out the contents and looked incredulously at the two fifty dollar bills.

"What the fuck," he said, "Where would he have got all this cash?"

The other officer looked just as astonished. The cash was put back into Mighty Mouth's pocket as he was handcuffed behind his back and then officers linked their arm with one of Mighty Mouth's and pulled him away. His knees and feet bounced off each step down two flights of stairs and then dragged along behind him as the officers yanked his dead weight away to twelve building where he would be placed in a segregation cell until he went to 'court' and his punishment decided.

23

William sent a note and a bag of commissary items to both Candy and Sparkle. The note informed them that they were now owned by William and that they would be taken care of rather than abused. William suggested that they continue as normal but to let him know of any issues they had with clients. Sparkle replied, thanking William and highlighting the problem clients and explained that everybody had been complaining about the prices rising. He described the abuses that Candy had endured at the hands of named inmates and a particular officer. William sent a note back to Sparkle with specific instructions about the ill-treating officer.

William was walking to medical to collect his daily dose of medication as Lieutenant Hardy bellowed down the hallway, telling

William to stop, put his hands against the wall and spread his legs. William complied without saying a word and smiled to himself. He knew what was on the cards. Lieutenant Hardy gave William a pat down, disappointed that he found nothing compromising.

"I'll be expecting the same arrangement to continue that I had with the previous owner," declared Hardy.

"Then you're going to be mighty disappointed." countered William.

"Do you want me to make things difficult for you?" Hardy challenged.

"I don't give a fuck, do what you want to do. You will anyway you pussy-ass bitch." William said as he walked off.

Lieutenant Hardy watched, staring at William's back considering his next options. He loathed that fucking Mad Dog.

"Wait up Mother-fucker," Hardy called after him.

William stopped and smiled as he turned round, looked at Hardy but remained mute. Hardy walked up to William.

"How much and how do you you want paying? Burger King, Subway sandwich, fried chicken?" Hardy said.

"Fifty dollars a time in cash or dope," said William.

"Fuck off Mad Dog, that is an extortionate price and I'm not bringing cash or drugs into the unit," said Hardy, his face twisting as he spoke.

"Don't get holier than fucking thou on me Hardy. You know the price is higher because you are an officer, and because you are a bad one. Plus, I hate you, so there is extra for that and you know that you don't need to bring anything into the unit. You fucking confiscate enough of it in shake-downs when you know someone has a stash. So it's not even fucking costing you anything to get your stinking dick sucked."

Hardy looked at William and smirked As he said, "No problem."

As William was about to leave, he pointed his finger in Hardy's face, his voice low and gruff as he said, "There'll be no fucking abusing my girls either."

"Mad Dog, you can take the fun out of anything," Hardy said.

William turned his back and walked away again.

Candy came and seated himself at William's table, fear on his face as he said, "Hardy has called me over to minor court."

"Ok, come and see me when you are back."

William had expected the request as Lieutenant Hardy had called in on him earlier in the day to pay him.

Candy went to the desk for a pass to go to court. There was no disciplinary case, but the room Hardy used wasn't in use, so he used it as his preferred place for abusing his 'girl' of choice. Hardy had no intention of complying with William's instruction of going gentle, especially as he was paying an extortionate price for his pleasure. Hardy was going to have his money's worth and gave Candy a sideways glance, the edges of his lips turning up slightly, as he came into the room.

An hour later Candy was back in the day-room and went over to William who wasn't looking well; pallid, not like Mad Dog at all.

"Are you ok Mad Dog?" Candy said, his face betraying concern.

"I'm fine. How was the asshole with you?"

"Even worse than before and I thought he was going to break my arm. I'm going to have bruises all over my back."

"Ok, go into my house, get a bottle of lotion, packet of chips and a candy bar. I won't be sending you to him again." William said.

Candy looked relieved, then a look of consternation came over his face.

"Won't he make things bad for me if I don't go when he calls me over?"

"Candy, how fucking bad do you think your life can get? You're in a super-max prison being fucked by a dozen guys a day, and giving blow jobs to another dozen. It's not what you call a perfect life. Don't worry about Hardy, he's my problem," said William.

24

William wasn't feeling good.

He had been feeling off colour for days and hadn't noticed his lack of energy at first until the dizzy spells began. They caught him unaware, and it was then that he started to take notice.

Along the hallways, lines were painted on the floor guiding the inmates who were expected to walk between the wall and the line and not to step outside of it. William had received two minor cases for having breached the rule two occasions as he became disorientated, stepping away from the hallowed line.

William lowered himself onto his bunk, head in hands, elbows digging into his thighs. He had just returned from medical, having had another batch of blood taken. He had seen the provider about his failing liver as a result of Hepatitis C, but he wasn't concerned with that right now. It was his huge testicle, the size of a grapefruit and now black in colour. It was throbbing intensely and sending shooting pains throughout his body. The intensity of the pain made him vomit and he jumped up to throw up in the toilet but it made his suffering worse, feeling light-headed with waves of dizziness.

William was thinking murderous thoughts about the Chinese doctor who he had asked to take a look at his huge ball but the doctor refused, telling him that he was there to see him about his liver, that was all. The doctor examined William, informing him that he was looking washed out but didn't ask why, or how William was feeling.

William was retching, nothing in his stomach to bring up but nevertheless couldn't stop. At this rate he would have no stomach lining left and he was vomiting blood, lots of it. Finally, he managed to stand upright again but his stomach was having spasms signalling another bout of retching. He leaned against the wall as he experienced a wave of dizziness with bouncing stars sparkling in front of his eyes.

"Mad Dog, you've got a visitor," shouted the desk officer.

William looked up in surprise. *Who would be visiting me, no one ever visits me?* He washed his face with cold water and brushed his teeth then walked over to the desk for his pass to meet his visitor.

William went through the routine of stripping off, squatting and coughing, then dressed again. He walked through the door into the visitation room and spotted his mother seated at the allocated table. She had already been to the vending machine and bought him three bags of tortilla chips, a coke. root beer and a Honeybun pastry.

"What the fuck are you doing here?" William said as his mother jumped up and gave him a hug. Whilst her hand was round the back of his neck she dropped a small tightly wrapped package down the back of his shirt. William sat quickly so that it wouldn't fall straight down his trouser leg and onto the floor. It was an unexpected gift, but William was a lightening fast thinker.

On the pretext of pulling up his pants, William retrieved the package which he kept hidden in the palm of his hand as he opened the wrapper on his Honeybun. Whilst his mother was chatting to him, telling him gossip from the streets, he broke a piece off the pastry. As he put it in his mouth he manoeuvred the package into his mouth too. After swallowing it down with a swig of coke he asked her how many of the little packages she had brought.

"Twenty in total," she replied.

William nodded. Her visit had been out of the blue for him, but it coincided with her needing regular medication for her heart. She didn't have medical insurance and had sent him a letter telling him about her situation. His dad was buying his own heart medication but wouldn't buy them for his wife. William had told his numerous clients on the unit where their family members had to send the money needed to pay for their weekly supply of drugs. The family member would pay his mother then she would buy the drugs and give them to someone else who would be visiting their loved one. He would then pass the goods onto William in return for a percentage of the cash or drugs he brought to William.

She had been passing him the little balled packages and he swallowed each one followed by a swig of his coke.

Whether it was talk of his loser brother that caused it he didn't know but William suddenly turned white as a sheet and felt faint.

"What's wrong with you boy?"

"It's nothing, it's just one of my balls, it's a bit swollen, gives me a bit of pain sometimes," William said.

"Stupid question, but have you seen the provider about it?"

"Of course, the fucking Chinese dick-sucker of a doctor told me I need to jack off and it will be ok," William told her.

"Let me see it. "

"Fuck no, it's fine."

"Let me fucking see it now," she said as she stood and walked around to William's side of the table.

William knew there was no point protesting and he pulled the waistband of his pants and boxer shorts out in front of him so that she could see his huge black testicle.

"What the fuck," she said and then turned to the officer walking around the visitation room, "You, get the warden in here, now."

"The warden is busy, he doesn't come into visitation unless there is a problem."

"Well there is a fucking problem you dumb bitch, call him over now," she said, spittle spraying as she spoke into his face, despite being a good foot shorter than him.

Everyone in the visiting room at this point had stopped talking and was watching William's mother make a scene.

"Ma'am, you need to quieten down, you are being disruptive and disturbing everyone else's visit," said Officer Donovan who was doing some easy weekend overtime in visitation.

"I don't give a fuck about anyone else, do I look like I give a fuck about anyone else? I only give a fuck that TDCJ is trying to kill my boy by not letting him see a doctor and be treated. Have you seen the size of his ball? Boy, show him your ball," she said as she turned back to William.

"No, no, no, don't do that. I'll call the warden to come down here."

"Well that's fucking better," she said. "Why didn't you fucking do that when I first fucking told you to do it asshole."

"Ma'am," said the old female officer on the desk, "I've called for the warden to come over, he's on his way but you need to calm down."

"Don't tell me to calm down you worthless ass bitch. All you mother-fuckers are trying to kill my boy and you tell me to calm down. Fuck you bitch."

"Ma'am, you will have to leave if you don't calm down," said the old officer know as Twinkle-toes as she was always dashing around everywhere. It was a challenge for her to be on desk duty as she didn't like to stay still.

"I'm not going anywhere until I've seen the warden," said William's mother.

"He's on his way, but you need to calm down and be quiet. Please sit down."

"Don't tell me to sit down and be quiet bitch, I'm going to keep going off until my boy is seen by a doctor."

"You are being disruptive. If you don't shut up I'm going to have you escorted off the unit for being a security risk."

"Bitch, I'm not leaving so shut the fuck up yourself. You can be fucking sure I know the rules and this is no security issue, this is a fucking medical issue. Now go and sit your worthless ass down. Where is the fucking warden?"

The warden had entered the visitation room and heard the last part of the rant by William's mother. William was taking no notice of what was going on and was talking to the inmate at the next table, telling him that his mother had always been this bad.

The warden had taken a cursory look around the room before addressing the crazy foul-mouthed woman in front of him.

"Ma'am, what's the trouble, how can I help you?"

William's mother turned round when she heard someone new addressing her.

"I want to know why you are trying to kill my boy. Why hasn't he seen a doctor? Have you seen the size of his ball?"

"Ma'am, I have no control or authority over the medical department. Your son can put in an I-60 form requesting to go to medical to be seen. He will then be seen within ten days," explained the warden.

"Don't give me that fucking bullshit. His ball hasn't got to the size of a cantaloupe overnight. Boy, show him your ball."

William's mother turned round to him as she said this and grabbed hold of his arm to pull him up.

"There's no need to show me, there's nothing I can do about it," repeated the warden.

However, William being no stranger to controversy or one to shy away from drama smiled as he pulled his pants and boxers down just far enough for the warden and several others to see his goods on display.

"Fuck me," declared the warden. "Are you telling me that the doctor has not seen you about this?"

"He's seen it and knows about it but keeps telling me I need to jack off."

"What are you going to do about it warden?" said William's mother.

The warden walked over to the desk and picked up the phone and called for an emergency ambulance to come to the unit and take William to the local hospital.

"That's more like it," said William's mother, needing to have the last word.

William, his mother and the warden left the visiting room to wait for the ambulance to arrive.

25

William woke up in a hospital bed having just undergone surgery.

When he arrived at the hospital he had been seen immediately by the doctor. After a lengthy discussion with William about his testicle, the doctor spent several minutes berating the prison medical staff and in particular the doctor who refused to treat the problem. He was incredulous when William told him that the quack's solution to the swollen testicle was to masturbate.

"I've a good mind to report that doctor for this."

William shrugged As he said, "He'll be replaced by another incompetent doctor who doesn't give a shit because we are only inmates."

"Well this is the situation now. At some point you've pulled a muscle in your groin, probably from working out too hard." The doctor gave William a quizzical look.

"I did pull a muscle a couple of years ago"

"Ok, well this is what happened. A hydroseal burst, that is what keeps fluid out of the testicle. In your case, it went untreated so long that the testicle drowned which has caused cancer. We had to remove the affected testicle." The doctor looked at William for a moment wondering whether to tell him more. "If you had been treated within six months of it happening we could have saved your testicle."

William could see the anger on the doctor's face and thought for a moment about what the doctor had told him. William wasn't one for dwelling on the past. after all it's wasn't as if he could change the situation.

"Doc, don't worry about it. Thank you for sorting me out," said William

"That's not the end of it. You'll need five rounds of Chemotherapy starting tomorrow. You're going to be here for a while."

"Is the food better here than the out of date slop we get fed in prison?"

"I would think much better," the doctor said, a smile spreading across his face.

"Then I'm happy to stay as long as I need to," said William, breaking into a laugh.

"You're taking it well, most patients don't react this way."

"Doc, those mother-fuckers at the prison are trying to kill me off, if not with the slop they feed then by not giving me my prescribed medication. You are working to keep me alive. Why wouldn't I be happy with that?" William said.

"Take it easy William," the doctor said as he walked out of the room.

It took several days for William to retrieve all of the packages he'd swallowed during his mother's visit. He had found a hiding place for them in the hospital ward behind a vent near his bed. They should be safe there until he returned to the unit, he thought.

William had lost weight throughout his medical ordeal, especially over the couple of years that his testicle had grown. His adult weight had always been around two hundred and sixty pounds but, almost three months after his operation and chemotherapy treatments, he weighed only a hundred and thirty pounds. His ailments had taken a massive toll on his body, a shadow of his former self.

"Are you sending me back yet Doc?" said William as the doctor walked into the room to talk to him.

"William, you have lost half your body weight and I can't release you back to the prison until you are at least a hundred and eighty pounds."

"Fuck me Doc, that's a lot of fried chicken and pizza you need to bring me. Can't say I'm complaining though."

26

William was back on the unit and had taken up where he left off. His boys had taken care of business for him while he was in the hospital and his bank balance in the free world had increased nicely thanks to Angel depositing the cash through his mother. William hadn't wanted to let on who his own personal cash mules were and Angel's mother visited every week, bringing goodies in for her son to continue the lucrative family business on the unit. Angel's clientele were the Mexicans who were loyal to the cartel with many working for his father in the world, mostly as low level distributors. They were now the middle men selling to anyone on the unit and remained loyal to the cartel because there was no alternative. In return their families were taken care of whilst they were doing time.

William had been housed in the same building and pod but a different section so, to see the guys, he had to fall out of place. He would have himself moved as soon as he saw the right officer or could convince someone that the guys needed to move.

William looked around and saw Old Man Lang seated at a table reading a book.

"Good to see you back," William said to him patting him on the shoulder.

"You too Mad Dog. It's always quieter without you here causing drama."

William laughed as he looked up at three row to see the guys looking down on the day room and him.

"Hey Mad Dog, it's about time you got your lazy ass back here instead of leaving us to take care of your business," called out Rat.

William looked up and grinned as he said "There's no point keeping dogs and barking myself you worthless mother-fuckers. It's called delegating."

William bounced up the steps, but didn't reach the top, instead losing balance and toppling over. He landed awkwardly on his right wrist.

"What the fuck," said Lenny and Rat at the same time.

"Are you drunk Mad Dog?" Angel said.

"No, I'm not fucking drunk. I don't know what's going on, I keep falling over."

The three guys ran down the two flights of stairs to help William and, with Angel's assistance, William stood up and stared at his wrist, which was definitely not right. He could feel an intensifying pain coursing through it but that didn't bother him, he could handle any amount of pain, indeed he thrived on it. What really rankled was that his wrist was at an odd angle.

"It looks like you've broken it, Let me see it," said Lenny

Officer Donovan came into the day-room as an inspection of William's wrist was taking place and he dawdled over to see what was going on.

"Hey Donovan, what's up?" said William.

"What's happened to your wrist?"

"Nothing it,s fine."

"I need to talk to you. I'll walk you over to medical," said Donovan.

"Ok, let's go." William said and looked at the guys who shrugged as he followed a distracted Donovan.

"What's going on Donovan?" William said as they walked down the hallway towards one building where medical was based.

"I need to make more money," said Donovan.

William smiled to himself and wasn't surprised at what Donovan was saying. It had happened with every single one of his mules over the years. They started out small, then a few months in they saw their bank balances grow and started spending, dreaming of fancy cars, holidays or houses.

"No problem at all. Instead of the two baggies a week, bring me two baggies every time you come on shift. That's eight baggies a week. Will that get you what you want?"

William was surprised at Donovan as he'd always appeared cautious, now been overtaken by greed. That worked fine for William. The more the better.

"Aren't you going to ask why?" Donovan asked.

"No, I don't care. That's your business."

"Your wrist looks broken." Donovan said as they walked through the door into medical.

"Can you get me moved back over to the section with my home-boys?" William said.

"I'll see what I can do now. I'll come and find you when I've sorted it. Thanks Mad Dog."

William was seen by one of the lazy nurses who roughly checked his wrist. Even for someone who thrived on pain as William did, he flinched.

"Fucking bitch, try being a gentle nurse instead of a fucking …

Lieutenant Hardy came through the door just as William was cursing the nurse.

"Fucking Mad Dog, everywhere I fucking go, there you are."

"Maybe I'm your conscience," William said, then adding, "Oh no, I forgot, you don't have one."

"Fuck you, Mad Dog, Why are you here?" he looked at William's misshapen wrist and accused him of fighting.

"Get off the fucking bullshit, asshole. I haven't been fighting. I fell out."

Lieutenant Hardy took out his notebook and started writing in it.

"I'm giving you a case for fighting."

"I wasn't fucking fighting, I told you, I fell out."

"So I'll change it to failure to keep yourself safe whilst drunk and high," said Hardy, his eyes Narrowing, following with, "Don't think you can barter your way out of this one either by buying commissary for whoever is running UCC."

"You'd know all about that wouldn't you Hardy? There's no one worse for the bribes and back-handers than you. I'll get the case dropped, you can be sure of that."

"Fuck you ass-hole," said Hardy as he left again.

Nurse Lazy came back with a bandage and strapped up his wrist then, before she was given more abuse about her ungentle ways, told him to leave. He was about to depart when Nurse Carling entered, glanced at his wrist and the poorly wrapped bandage.

"How did you hurt your wrist?" said Nurse Carling as she re-strapped it. "I guess it was fighting, you look the type."

"Well thanks for the compliment Carling but no, I wasn't fighting. I fell over going up the stairs. It's happened a few times since I came out of the hospital."

Nurse Carling opened the computer screen and checked Williams medical file, spending a few minutes reading his notes.

"Well no wonder you keep falling over."

William looked at her bemused.

"When you have a testicle removed, it alters your balance. It's like your big toes, they are for balance too. When you had it removed, they should have put a counter weight in there but they haven't done that. Plus you should be having physical therapy to help with re-balancing."

Nurse Carling tapped away at the computer for a minute. "Ok, I have put your name on the list for therapy and prioritised you as urgent."

"Thank you very much, I appreciate it," said William, his eyes wide with shock.

"Why are you so surprised?"

"I have been in this prison system for years and you are the first medical person I've met who's competent, appears to care."

"Really? That is what doctors and nurses do."

"Not here. Generally the ones who work in prison are unemployable elsewhere. Anyway I appreciate you taking care of me."

"You're welcome."

She took another long look at his file and said, "How are you feeling with the post op medication."

"Ok, not great. Why?

"You are not being given any of the medications you were prescribed," she said and followed with, "TDCJ won't pay for those drugs, they only give their own versions or general painkillers. Let me know if you feel worse."

"Good old TDCJ, always making sure to fuck over the inmates," said William, disgust evident in his face as he continued, "Can you write on my file, the reason I fell out? That mother-fucker Hardy has given me a case for it."

Nurse Carling looked William up and down, dwelling a long time on the space between his legs, as she said, "You could do something for me too."

William grinned as they went into the office and she locked the door.

27

"Mad Dog, that bastard Hardy has called for me again," said Candy with a tremor of fear in his voice.

"Ok, don't worry about it, I'm not sending you," William said. "Go and tell Sparkle I want to talk to him."

Sparkle came from his cell where he had just finished servicing his morning clientele, the inmates who worked at night and a couple of officers. His time was his own until the afternoon, when early shift and school finished. He sat at the table, opposite William.

"What's up Mad Dog," he said as he pulled his long silky black hair back into a ponytail.

"I want you to go and see Hardy instead of Candy and let him do what he wants. He'll get rough, but I want you to let him do that to you," William told him.

Sparkle didn't look pleased and William knew what he was thinking.

"Don't worry, it's just this once. We are going to rid ourselves of that sadistic asshole. Come and see me as soon as you get back."

Lieutenant Hardy was unhappy when Sparkle came to see him instead of Candy. He liked Candy because he was a pushover and derived pleasure from beating him because Candy was weak, never retaliating. So far, neither had that mother-fucker Mad Dog, despite insisting that there would be no abuse.

During the session, Sparkle endured what Candy normally did and was shocked at the level of violence Candy had tolerated; unsurprising that he would become worked up and stressed when he knew he had to see Hardy. Candy had never confided in anyone what went on. Sparkle went straight to William's table and sat down gently, his rear tender and William saw Sparkle wince. He called Candy over to listen as Sparkle told William in graphic detail what Hardy had done.

"Is that what he's been doing to you every time, Candy?"

Candy looked at his shoes as his eyes welled up with tears and nodded his confirmation.

"Why didn't you tell me it was so bad? I'd never have let it carry on so long."

William rose from the table and strolled to his cell, returning with an armful of commissary, including candy bars, chips and two bottles of body lotion. He gave it to Candy and a weak smile spread across his face

"Let me know what you want from commissary and I'll get it next time I go," said William.

"Thanks Mad Dog," Candy said and William watched him walk away dressed in his home made sports bra and skin-tight trousers, hair scraped back and plastered down into a short pigtail.

"Right Sparkle, I want you to write a kite, outlining everything Hardy has just done. At shift change, you're going to give it to Officer Donovan and you can be sure he'll take it seriously."

28

There was a new officer on the pod, tall, black and sweating profusely. He was carrying a lot more weight than was good for him and wore a coloured scarf round his neck to dry off his sweaty face. The colours on the scarf were significant as it told others the identity of the gang to which he belonged. The officer scanned around the pod as the inmates stopped what they were doing to stare at him.

"You, white boys," the officer shouted, using a derogatory term for white inmates, exposing a mouth full of gold teeth in the process. "Get off the phone during count."

The officer turned to a group of black inmates seated at a table playing dominoes and made a hand signal, reciprocated by the inmates.

"What are you doing here Roscoe?" NJ asked, so called for originating from New Jersey, "Last time I saw you was at my brother's funeral, when he got shot up in that rival drive-by."

"Got transferred for beating up too many pussy-ass white boys," he said, a chuckle rising in his throat, "Left a couple of them permanently drooling at the mouth."

The dominoes players laughed, then spent a few minutes catching up on what was happening with their fellow gangsters in the free-world. There were always battles and 'wars' going on between gangs, often spilling over into prison, and vice versa. Roscoe told them of the latest situation taking place between their gang and a prominent white gang. They were always over territory, prices and the availability of drugs and Roscoe warned the inmates to be ready for a fight to happen in the unit soon. The dominoes players peered at each other, some in excited anticipation, others weary of having to fight again, and a few apprehensive at the thought, but knowing that their participation was expected.

"White boys," Roscoe shouted again as he strode over to the inmates in question."Are you deaf as well as stupid, you dumb mother-fucker pussies?"

Roscoe knew what he was doing and took perverse pleasure in demeaning white inmates at every opportunity. He also enjoyed creating trouble any way he could. Roscoe had become a correctional officer for three reasons: one, he had never been caught for any of his crimes, two, he could help his fellow 'brothers' in the gang and this had been endorsed by the gang leaders as they felt that it was prudent to have members working as officers, and three, he could use his power over inmates to do whatever he wanted to them. Number three was his favourite and he made the most of it.

Roscoe looked at both of the inmates using their phone. Neither were well built. One had a commanding demeanour so he turned to the other one and grabbed the front of the inmates t-shirt with both hands, hoisting him off a round metal stool that was fixed to the floor.

"Are you a little punk bitch?" Roscoe spat in his face.

Blaine, the inmate being assaulted, was outraged at having hands put on him. Despite his unassuming appearance, he was a feisty character and not without influence. He was a second cousin of Angel's.

"Get your filthy monkey hands off me, you fucking deranged black mother-fucker," snarled Blaine.

"What are you going to do if I don't."

Blaine, who was nicknamed The Ferret in his junior boxing days, didn't hesitate and grabbed hold of Roscoe's ears and followed with a head-but. Then, he pulled Roscoe's head to one side, clamped his teeth around the top part of Roscoe's ear and bit as hard as he could, grinding his teeth. He didn't ease up until he felt the upper part of Roscoe's ear tear away. Blaine spat out the ear in disgust, blood running down his chin. He spat the blood from his mouth.

As soon as Roscoe lifted Blaine off the stool, Rat dropped the phone and placed his hands either side of the stool, pushed himself forward and kicked out at the side of Roscoe's knee. He didn't achieve the impact he wanted, aiming to break the joint. Roscoe had shifted his position slightly as Blaine head-butted him. Rat took full advantage of the situation as Roscoe was now facing Rat head on, Blaine's back to him, legs dangling. That left Rat a clear shot as he kicked Roscoe in the groin with all of the force he could muster. Rat wasn't able to assess how much the impact had hurt Roscoe due to the piercing screams caused by the officer having his ear bitten off. Rat took this as a cue to inflict a couple more brutal kicks to the groin. Roscoe fell to his knees as Blaine was spitting his ear out of his mouth.

Rat held his hand out to Blaine to help him up off the floor and they headed back to their cells, Blaine telling Rat that he would need to shower for a week to feel clean again. Roscoe's gangster friends scowled at Roscoe's assailants, hurling insults, but doing little else to help Roscoe, not wanting to be caught up in the inevitable investigation.

29

"Mad Dog, I've just heard trouble is escalating between the blacks and the whites. The blacks are trying to claim that the territory the whites have been working, is theirs. We supply these particular whites with their product, so the territory needs defending. The fight is coming to our door and we need to be ready," said Angel.

They were in the chow hall eating lunch even though it was eight o'clock in the morning. Meal times were often ridiculous: Breakfast was at three in the morning and dinner at two in the afternoon. They were seated at the table with four of Angel's crew, talking about the trouble heading their way.

As William and Angel arrived back into their pod, they walked into a highly strung and excited area. Everyone was buzzing as they talked about what had just happened. William and Angel raised their head to watch a congregation of inmates at Blaine's door. They jogged up the stairs and pushed their way through the dozen or more guys laughing as Blaine regaled them with the story of Roscoe's ear detachment. Blaine spotted William and Angel and beckoned them to come to his door. This time he didn't embellish, telling the story straight, as it had transpired. Blaine knew that there would be repercussions and he warned Angel told Blaine about the war brewing, telling them that needed to prepare.

Angel paused in thought for a moment And then said, "Mad Dog, why don't you and the whites join up with us for this fight? It serves both our purposes; we have backing from the Peckerwoods (whites) against retaliating and we have the numbers to back you in the free-world war.

"Good idea," said William, nodding in approval, "We'd better get the word out about getting tooled up."

As they were discussing their plan a commotion started at the door as the ninja turtles arrived and strode towards the stairs.

"Blaine, we've plenty of guys in seg. They'll take care of what you need until you get your property. I'll pack up all your shit, don't want those thieving mother-fucker officers breaking or confiscating your stuff."

"Thanks Angel, I guess I'll miss the fight. You take those mother-fuckers down," he said and a grinned decorated his face as he continued, "Not my first and won't be my last stint in seg,"

Like William, he considered being in segregation to be an inconvenience, no more, part and parcel of life in prison.

The ninja's reached the door and shoved William aside.

"Hey you fat mother-fucker, keep your bitch-ass sweaty hands to yourself. Do not touch me," said William at the ninja who has panting like a dog due to the three hundred pounds of excess blubber he carried.

He was not the only member of the ninja turtles to carry such weight and Ninja number one wisely decided to ignore William, turning to the task in hand. He hadn't become part of the ninja turtle team by being blind, deaf and dumb to a potentially volatile situation. If William had reacted instinctively to being shoved by punching the officer, all hell would have let loose in the pod. The ninjas would have been overpowered by inmates and dealt with harshly.

"Back up to the door with your hands behind your back to be cuffed," shouted number one Ninja.

"Fuck you, asshole," replied Blaine.

"This is your second warning mother-fucker. Make it easy on yourself," shouted number two Ninja.

"You know you're coming out one way or another," shouted Ninja number one again. "There's no need for you to get hurt if you follow instructions."

"Fuck you," answered Blaine. "You know I'm not going to reach medical without a lot of bruises and maybe a broken bone or two that you fuckers will give me."

"We don't work like that," said Ninja number two, rolling his eyes, "Now back up to the door with your hands behind your back."

"Bullshit, you lying piece of shit. That video camera you have recording everything will conveniently have a section missing after you've doctored it. You do it all the time."

Ninja number one and two looked at each other for a lingering moment, the time filled with unsaid meaning.

"If you don't back up to the door, I'm going to gas you," threatened Ninja number two.

"Who gives a fuck asshole, I don't, but I'm not going to make your job easier for you."

At this point Blaine's cellie chimed in and said, "I don't want to be gassed because of you, just do as they say."

"Fuck you, coward ass mother-fucker."

"This is your second warning, are you coming out quietly?" Ninja number two asked.

"Fuck no," answered Blaine with a cheeky grin.

Ninja number one took out the canister of pepper spray from his belt and sprayed the gas through the door hatch into Blaine's cell.

"Thanks for nothing," whined Blaine's cellie as the pair of them choked and spluttered.

"Have you had enough?" Ninja number two asked.

"Hell no, you think that bit of spray is going to bother me, plus my delicate little cellie here has never been gassed so I'm doing it for him."

"Ok, here it comes," said Ninja number one as he sprayed the gas into the cell again, this time spraying for twice as long.

Blaine and his cellie were on the floor gasping for breath and cellie made the mistake of rubbing his eyes, intensifying the burning ten-fold. It was already making his skin bristle and he felt the urge to scratch all over. Ninja number one opened the cell door and all seven piled in, following their number order, the cameraman at the back, recording everything. In general, Ninja's one to five were responsible for restraining a limb and head, whereas Ninja number six cuffed the suspect and, in some cases, shackled the feet. They pulled Blaine up to his feet.

"Are you going to walk, or cause any more trouble," asked Ninja two.

"What the fuck do you think," he said as a long strand of drool stretched like elastic from the corner of his mouth down to his knees, threatening any moment to cut free from it's tether. Another two hung from each nostril. "No I'm not going to walk, and yes I'm going to give you more trouble."

The ninjas grinned as ninja one pushed Blaine out of the door and numbers one to four picked him up and carried him horizontally backside up, down the steps. At the last minute, ninja seven remembered the cellie and sent numbers five and six to escort him over to medical to be cleaned up and treated for the effects of the pepper spray.

Everyone was laughing and cheering for Blaine as he was carried off the pod.

"You know he's related to me don't you," Angel said to William.

William looked at Angel in surprise.

"Yeah, he's a cousin. Need to look after him. We had him work as liaison between us and the whites. It's like he was born to it," he said and laughed.

Officer Donovan came on the pod with a new air of confidence about him. He had the makings of a good and fair officer, although under William's thumb it couldn't be any different. The job was proving lucrative for him, managing to buy a couple of year old truck as he didn't want to raise any red flags. Donovan didn't want to end up like his friend who had talked him into the job. He had been busted bringing drugs into his unit and had been walked off the premises. The guy was lucky only to have lost his job; he could easily have been arrested, charged and ended up serving time amongst those he had served as a mule. Donovan's friend had been too extravagant with his cash and it had been noticed.

Donovan was saving furiously for a house, one on a new housing estate being built. He'd managed to put a hefty deposit on one and, by the time it was built, he would have enough to pay the balance in full. For now, he was happy residing in a nice new luxury travel trailer he'd purchased on a two acre plot of land he had bought in the middle of nowhere for a few hundred dollars. On the advice of William, Donovan had been putting a good chunk of money as a future pension plan and emergency money should anything go wrong.

The pod was calm and Donovan didn't feel the need to alter that. He didn't bother about sheets up across doors, clothes hanging out drying on the run or guys indulging in a bit of gambling. William had schooled him well, explaining about the lives of inmates and why things were the way that they were.

It's a difficult and often dangerous environment to live in, don't make it worse because you want to be an asshole.

Donovan could see the value in William's advice and it wasn't in his nature to make life harder for anyone, least of all himself.

He was at a desk reading a book that one of the inmates had lent him, when he saw one of the she-males approach.

"What time is it?" Sparkle said.

Donovan looked up at the clock on the wall and, as he did, Sparkle dropped the kite on the desk.

"Two twenty."

"Thanks," said Sparkle and wandered off.

That was weird.

As he looked back down at his book, a tiny folded square of paper caught his eye. He placed his book on the table and picked up the note. After unfolding it, he read the contents and his expression changed to one of horror. He glanced over to Sparkle's cell but saw no one. However, William was now standing in-front of him.

William had given the nod to Sparkle a few minutes after Donovan had come in and watched the exchange. There was a reason that William had suggested Donovan as the officer to trust for he had plans for Donovan, involving setting him up as a Sergeant.

"That kite you just got, what are you going to do about it?"

"I don't know, what am I supposed to do? Give it to the shift captain I guess." Donovan said, his gaze distant, suggesting that he was unsure.

"You can do and he might investigate. Tell him you found the kite, not that it was given to you. Or, you could investigate it yourself, then pass the report on to the shift captain. That will look good for you."

"You think I should?"

"Of course, why else would I have said it, asshole? When you go to lunch, call him out for something and take him to an unused room to get a full statement from him. Then attach the kite to it and give it to the shift captain."

"Thanks Mad Dog, appreciate it."

William sauntered back to his table where he had been playing cards with some of the guys.

Two hours later he saw Donovan leave the pod and five minutes later Sparkle followed. They came back separately an hour later and Donovan glanced over at William and nodded. Sparkle walked past William and winked as William smiled.

They were racked up again and William was reading a book he'd borrowed from Rat about the French aristocracy. He could see why Rat liked them so much. There was everything in them: Murder, deceit, conspiracies, adultery, intrigue and death by guillotine. His cellie was snoring on his bunk and William stood so that he could poke him, not because it stopped him snoring but it left a series of bruises on the cellie and he was never sure how they came about. That amused William greatly. As he returned to his bunk, William spotted a kite drift under his door, attached to the end of a piece of string made from the elastic from a pair of boxer shorts, the common method of creating chord to send messages, food and other things from one cell to another. William was a master at it, having spent plenty of time in segregation where he could hone his skills. He picked the kite up and read it.

Had enough of this shithole? Tonight's the night. Sign below.

There were already five bunk numbers written on it.

Fuck that, thought William and sent the kite to the next cell.

These types of kites came around periodically when the atmosphere in the unit became heavy and despondent. Inmates, usually but not exclusively, became sick of the abuse and mind games being played from all sides: Inmates, officers and administration. Prison life was designed to be difficult, especially for inmates. TDCJ had a punishment policy, making it difficult even for those inmates who tried to keep their nose clean, avoiding trouble or confrontation most of the time. The system encouraged antagonism and discord and revelled in it's punitive mindset. In addition, there were the prison politics and code of conduct between inmates. The line blurring as old school criminals, who lived by strict codes, became fewer and more undisciplined youngsters, who knew nothing about codes, become more prevalent. This created animosity between the different inmate classes. The hierarchy of inmates, dependent on the severity of their crimes was also a factor. Murderers were top dog, with sex offenders being the scourge of the inmate population. Different facets of prison life influenced the thoughts, actions and decisions of inmates.

"What the fuck," said William as the full lights came on. He looked at the clock on his radio, it was not even four am.

He heard shouting on the pod and rose to see what was happening. There were a dozen officers on the pod, each one frantically going from cell to cell checking everyone was alive. They were shouting for everyone to wake up and bring their identification to the door. William asked Officer Stead what was going on.

"Thirteen swingers, all dead," he explained as he marked William and Spider off on his clipboard.

William glanced across at the day-room to the cells on the other side. Two officers were cutting down one body whilst his cellie was seated at a table in the day-room. William spotted one inmate still swinging up on two row.

"Nothing to get excited about Spider, may as well go back to sleep."

Spider stayed at the door watching and saw two of the laws lay the body of his co-worker and, dare he say it, friend, down on the floor. A tear rolled down his cheek and he wiped it away but a moment later he was sobbing.

32

Several new inmates moved into cells recently vacated by those who had hanged themselves. One of them aroused great interest.

"Is that the Eyeball killer?" said one inmate.

Another confirmed his identity, saying that he had been on a previous unit with him. There were mutterings circulating about how the murderer had surgically removed the eyeballs from each of the women he'd killed. Sensationalist killers were often viewed in awe by other inmates and it was certainly the case with this one. The Eyeball Killer had a team of five officers laden down with boxes of his paperwork following him to his newly allocated cell. Unlike other inmates, he was in a cell on his own, purely because he had so much legal documents. It was a source of frustration to the administration that they could not order him to dispose of legal texts and this prisoner liked his documents in order, barking instructions to the officers about where to place each box. Irritated, the officers followed instructions, then departed quickly. The inmate made himself a cup of coffee, popped his door open and exited into the day-room then sat down at a table with one other white man already seated. He looked up and introduced himself.

"I'm Charlie," he said and held out his hand.

"I'm Mad Dog," replied William, taking his hand and shaking it, noticing that Charlie had a solid handshake; he liked that.

"Mad Dog huh. I've heard your name a lot. You give the laws a run for their money."

William laughed uproariously, then said, "I do my best. I aim to break a rule every day and make those lazy-ass mother-fuckers work for their pay-check. If they insist on keeping me here, then they have to earn it. I tell them all the time that they should be thanking me everyday for having a job to come to."

"I like the way you think Mad Dog," Charlie said and chuckled.

"I like how those clowns have to carry your legal shit when they decide to move you. I bet you have them carrying all kinds of contraband in it."

"You have no idea," said Charlie, "I get a real kick out of that. I presently have two shanks amongst my papers."

"The Eyeball Killer huh," William said and looked at him thoughtfully.

"That's what they call me," Charlie said, studying William in return, adding "My legal paperwork is a safe storage facility and I charge a reasonable fee."

William looked at him and nodded contemplatively before saying, "I think that's very interesting Charlie, let me think about it."

William was being his usual cautionary self, but he knew instinctively that The Eyeball Killer was someone he could trust, at least within the prison environs.

Donovan knocked on the door of Captain Mauser's office and waited.

"Come in, come in," a jovial voice called out.

Donovan entered and stood in front of the blond haired man of six foot five inches. Even sat he seemed as tall as Donovan was standing up. Donovan stood to attention feeling nervous.

"Officer Donovan, what can I do you for," Mauser asked in a sing-song voice with a hint of an accent that Donovan couldn't identify. Judging by his name, it was possible that Captain Mauser was of Germanic extraction.

"Take a seat, make yourself comfortable."

"Captain, I want to bring you my report on an investigation I've performed," Donovan said glancing down at his feet, out of his league addressing the Captain.

"Is that right, well let me take a look," Mauser said as he took the paperwork from Donovan's hand.

Captain Mauser took his time reading the contents, finally peering up at Donovan before looking down to read the report again.

"Did this inmate give you the kite?" Mauser asked.

"No, I found it. I think it had been dropped."

Donovan kept his answer purposely vague.

"Excellent work Donovan, excellent indeed. You'll be promoted to Sergeant for this. I will be putting you forward for promotion most definitely."

Donovan blushed and thanked the captain.

"I'm glad you brought this directly to me. I shouldn't tell you this Donovan but I despise Lieutenant Hardy, always has been a bully, no matter how many reprimands he's had. I will handle this. Great work Donovan."

Three days later Donovan was on the pod again and went over to William's cell to speak to him.

"Hardy has been transferred to a different unit but he's kept his rank, they were short of LT's," said Donovan with a grin.

"And is Captain Mauser recommending you for sergeant?" William said, glancing down and smiling.

"Yes he is, I can't believe it. He told me I'd done an excellent job with the investigation."

"That is exactly why I told you to do it as you did. Captain Mauser is a straight up officer, I've known him forever. He's worked on two other units that I've been on. I also know he hates Hardy and knew you'd get a promotion out of it."

"Thanks Mad Dog. I don't know what to say."

"Then don't. It's beneficial for us both and I didn't just do it for you. As a sergeant, you'll be able to move around the building as you want, it will make business easier for us."

"Thanks again Mad Dog." Donovan said as he walked back to the desk.

William had just returned from medical where he had given more blood for more tests. He had also spent a satisfactory fifteen minutes with Nurse Carling, locked in her office, both leaving the room with smiles on their faces. For William there was an upside to having health issues and the need to come to medical everyday. Not only did he get regular sex, Nurse Carling was bringing him everything he asked of her. Plenty of drugs, food from a collection of restaurants and fast food places, messages to and from people in the free world and, today, a quart of whiskey. He would give her cash to take out of the unit and deposit in his bank. He had tested her with a small amount at first and she had passed, so he would entrust her with larger amounts regularly. He had warned her of the consequences if she snitched on him or cheated him but Nurse

Carling was far too smitten with William to consider doing that. Even though she was proving to be a useful supply chain, she was certainly not his only route.

"Mad Dog, I need some more," said a familiar voice behind him.

William turned round to face Sam, a tall skinny white man, sixty years old, with ravaged features from years of heroin abuse. His hollow eyes gave him a haunted look.

"Sam, you already owe two hundred dollars," said William. He had to remind him every time he came looking for a fix.

"You know I have money Mad Dog. Please I really need a fix."

"Ok, but I'm cutting you off if you don't start paying your debt. I'll give you one month to pay up and, if you don't, then I'm cutting you off from the whole farm."

Sam knew what that meant. William would put the word out around the whole unit that nobody should supply Sam with drugs as he owed a large debt.

"You know my sister sends me money Mad Dog, you'll get it," said Sam as he wandered off happy at having another fix.

William turned back to the game of cards he was playing with the guys.

"I think I'm going to sell his debt on," mused William.

"I'll buy him from you, " said Angel, "I've seen him with his sister at visit, I know who she is."

"Give me seventy five dollars and he's yours," said William.

"Done."

"Sam, where is my money," shouted Angel across the day room to where Sam was begging a member of a black gang for a fix.

Angel stalked across the room. "Nobody will give you anything Sam. I put the word out to cut you off and your debt is three hundred and you haven't paid anything off."

"My sister sends me money, you'll get it." He said, repeating it like a mantra whenever his mounting debt was mentioned. He couldn't understand why his sister hadn't put the money in his account. She was a hundred percent reliable.

Angel gave an imperceptible nod to the two Carlos' seated at a table watching the exchange. They stood, went over to Sam, taking one arm each and walked him over to the shower block. Sam didn't resist, mostly because he was too spaced out to realise what was happening. The two Mexicans pushed him into a shower stall, taking turns to rain blows on Sam, avoiding his face, arms and legs, though it seemed he already had two black eyes. This was a roughing up, not a full on beating, a warning.

The Mexicans left Sam seated on a toilet to recover and had been scared to hit too hard. The addict was thin and fragile from his drug abuse, breaking his bones would have been too easy; those were not the orders of their boss. As it was, they left plenty of bruises and a few sore muscles.

Angel waited another week; still there was no money forthcoming and he couldn't let it ride any longer. He had a professional and personal reputation to think of, though it gave him no great pleasure to deal with sad cases like Sam's. It would send the wrong message to his other clients if he didn't follow through and, this time, he wouldn't forewarn Sam.

Sam was walking down the hallway, heading for outside recreation. He made frequent stops to lean against the wall, clutching his side in pain.

"Hey inmate, get off the wall and keep moving. What's wrong with you?" said a Mexican officer named Ortiz.

Sam started walking again, slowly, with a visible limp.

"Inmate, have you been fighting? Why do you have black eyes?" Ortiz said, inspecting Sam's face.

"No, no. I'm ok. There's nothing wrong with me."

"Well you look like you've been fighting. Come on, I'm taking you to medical to get checked out then to lock up. I'm writing you a case for fighting."

Sam didn't respond and walked with Officer Ortiz, still taking frequent rests against the wall. He was given an adequate check, which found that he had two broken ribs. An x-ray found that he also had a hairline fracture in his wrist. With his wrist strapped up and a couple of painkillers to ease the pain from the broken ribs, Ortiz escorted him to twelve building where he was placed in an administrative segregation cell.

"I need my property," Sam called out to Ortiz as he walked away.

"It will be packed up and brought over," replied Ortiz without turning around.

Hey Sam, are you ok?" said a voice from a neighbouring cell.

"I don't know, " Sam said, as he didn't know who was speaking.

The voice continued, "I got word from Angel that your sister is in hospital. She had a heart attack, but she's going to be ok."

"What? My sister had a heart attack? How do you know?"

Sam didn't want it to be true. His sister had looked after him his whole life, sent him to so many stints in rehab to no avail as Sam just kept on using. It was all he knew and he had frequently let her down, particularly this last time, landing back in prison for something stupid. He'd tried to rob a pharmacy in the middle of the day, pretending to be holding a gun in his pocket and had nodded out from the fix he had just taken before entering the store. He'd fallen over, hitting his head on the counter on his way to the floor and woken up in a hospital bed handcuffed to the bed frame.

Fortunately, he and his sister had money from a large payout they had received when he was a teenager. His sister, Mary, was ten years older than Sam and had been given custody of him when their parents had been killed by a drunk truck driver who had swerved and hit their car head on. Mary had taken good advice and invested money wisely and had retained a good lawyer to defend Sam in his trial. He had received a ten year sentence for his disastrous robbery attempt when the state prosecutor had pushed for twenty five years.

"Let's just say it's lucky our boys were with her when she had the heart attack."

Sam sat down on the bare steel bunk and cried.

Officer Ortiz came for Sam the following morning to be interviewed by STG, the unit's security threat group officers. Sam sat at the desk facing two officers.

"Sam, tell us how you received the injuries, were you fighting?" Sergeant Wood asked.

Sam looked down at his knees and shook his head.

"How did you get the broken ribs and the fractured wrist?"

"I fell off my bunk."

"Inmate," said Lieutenant Shandy, "if you are saying those injuries, two black eyes and bruises all over your body were from falling off your bunk, we don't believe it. Try again."

Sam didn't move his position or react. He was in a catch twenty two; if he said he'd been fighting he would receive a major case for it. If he said he owed a debt for buying drugs the result would be the same. Snitching about what really happened came with it's own set of undesirable consequences. Sam decided that his best strategy was to say nothing.

"Were you beaten up?" Sergeant Wood said again, "Sam we can't help you if you don't tell us what happened."

"I reckon you're being threatened by someone," said Lieutenant Shandy.

"Nothing happened, I fell off my bunk."

"Are you sure you don't want to say anything Sam? We have a good theory as to what really happened."

Sam said nothing, instead finding something interesting to stare at on the floor.

"Sam, it's your last chance, then we'll throw the book at you. We won't have a choice but we won't have to if you tell us what happened to you," said Sergeant Wood.

"My sister had a heart attack, and it's all my fault."

"How is it your fault Sam," Sergeant Wood said, wanting to coax and encourage Sam to talk more; feeling guilty was a good state of mind when extracting confessions.

"I owed a lot of money to someone and kept writing to my sister telling her to put more and more money on my books but she didn't put any money on there. I just kept harassing her for more money."

"Sam, I don't think you caused her heart attack. Who did you owe money to?"

Sam wouldn't answer this question. He had said enough. *So much for keeping his mouth shut*, he thought, but his emotions had overwhelmed him.

Neither Lieutenant Shandy's direct approach or Sergeant Wood's soft approach could convince Sam to identify to whom he owed the debt.

"Ok Sam, here's what we are going to do. You need to fill out this LID, Life in Danger form. We will then present that to UCC the unit classification committee. They will decide what will happen to you."

A few days later Sam found himself on chain being transferred to another unit but the debt would follow him. Angel would find out to where he'd been transferred; his people on the new unit would collect, that was a certainty.

"Mad Dog"

William didn't hear his name being spoken. He was experiencing a dizzy spell and was focusing on keeping his balance. He felt that familiar sensation in his stomach. He vomited blood over the floor.

"Mad Dog," the voice increased it's volume.

William thought he heard his name being called and opened his eyes, but had to wait for the blackness to clear before he could see anything. He looked around at his door to see Officer Stead peering in at him.

"Mad Dog, are you ok? You look terrible."

With some effort William managed to come off the wall and step over to the door where he promptly threw up more blood.

"Mad Dog, what the fuck is wrong with you?"

"I'm having a lot of pain in my liver," William said. "That Chinese butcher mother-fucker wouldn't even take a look."

"You look white as a sheet and puking blood is a bad sign." Stead said.

"Not the sheets here, they haven't seen white for twenty years," said William, ever the smartass.

"Maybe I should get you to ..." Officer Stead didn't have chance to finish the sentence as he watched William crumple and fall against the cell door. He was out cold.

"Mad Dog!" Stead shouted at William to no effect.

Officer Stead turned to look up at the officer in the picket.

"Get this door open now."

After seconds that felt like minutes, the door slid open and William fell out of the doorway as the door no longer held him in his collapsed position. Officer Stead shouted instructions to call for a nurse and gurney, bending down to try to revive William. Smacking his cheek didn't help so he checked William's pulse.

Weak, difficult to detect. He pulled up one of William's eyelids, witnessing his eyes rolled up into his head.

"No way, Mad Dog, you are not dying on me."

He gave William a short kick on his leg, aiming to illicit a reaction. Nothing. He pulled out his radio transmitter.

"Ambulance and now," he shouted to the person on the receiving end, "Get me an ETA."

By now, the guys in the day room realised something was going on, different to the usual dramas of idiots high on drugs, arguments between inmates or fights breaking out. A crowd built up around the cell with plenty of speculation as to what was happening.

"Fuck!" Goofy the tall lanky Latino exclaimed. "It's Mad Dog, he's out cold. Maybe Stead tasered him."

"Why the fuck would he do that?" Bulldog a short squat Mexican said.

"Get out of the way you mother-fuckers," shouted a voice, which put a temporary end to speculations. "Let us through."

A few of the men moved aside to let the two nurses through with the gurney, a male and female nurse, the only medical staff that would have been on duty over the holiday weekend.

"An hour for the ambulance to get here Stead," said the female nurse.

"Hell no, he doesn't have that long. He needs to get to the hospital now."

Officer Stead pushed the transmit button on his radio whilst supervising the two nurses hauling William onto the gurney. They were struggling with the size of him, so he instructed two of the watching inmates to help them.

"Get me a van to the medical entrance now," he shouted down the radio.

He listened for a moment to the response.

"Just do as I said," he shouted again, "I don't have time for your foolish questions. That van needs to be waiting and ready to roll for me to get this guy to the hospital."

Officer Stead didn't wait for the nurses to secure the patient before he grabbed hold of one end of the trolley and pulled it towards the door. The two nurses looked at each other and shrugged. They were not going to object to someone else doing their job.

"Keep up, " Officer Stead said as they trotted obediently behind pushing the gurney from either side.

They wheeled William out of the door to the waiting prisoner transport van. There was no room for the gurney between the seats so they had to lift William's dead weight into a seat. It took a lot of dragging, pushing to manoeuvre William's bulk into a seat. Officer Stead spotted Officer Huntley out of the corner of his eye as she stepped out of the drivers seat.

"Huntley, you're coming with me."

Huntley was startled at Stead's instruction but cottoned on to the situation instantly. Whilst Stead and the two nurses manhandled William into a seat, she ran to the medical office and lifted the phone. Huntley studied the list of external phone numbers printed out on a sheet which had been stuck up on the wall And called the number for the regional hospital, telling them to expect an inmate in the next ten minutes and that there was no time to wait for an ambulance. She ran back outside just as Officer Stead was shutting the rear doors to the van.

"Get in, I'll drive," she shouted.

Stead looked like he was about to object, then decided that there wasn't time and jumped in the passenger side. Huntley set off before he had even closed the door.

"I told the hospital we'll be there in ten minutes," she said.

"That'll be a miracle if we get there in ten, more like twenty."

"Looks like he's in need of a miracle. Let's do our best."

Officer Stead turned to look at the unresponsive William.

"Mad Dog, I'm trusting you not to try and escape, We are putting ourselves on the line for you so don't fuck up. If you attempt to escape, I'll tell them to shoot you dead. Do you hear me!"

Officer Huntley glanced at Stead as she said, "You know he can't hear you."

"He can hear me," said Stead.

Twelve minutes later Stead was looking white as a sheet and feeling sick as a dog. They screeched to a halt outside the ambulance entrance of the hospital. Stead had jumped into the back next to William to prevent him from being thrown all over the place. The last thing they needed was for William to have his head smashed from being hurled from his seat.

"Where the hell did you learn to drive?"

"He's still alive, that's what counts," said Huntley as Officer Stead grunted.

The hospital nurses were waiting at the door with gurney and a variety of instruments in hand. The speed with which they had had William onto the gurney and running down the hospital corridor was a triumph; it certainly didn't happen at the unit.

Officers Stead and Huntley were informed that they could be present in the examination room. By the time they reached it, the duty doctor was giving instructions for emergency surgery. William's medical records had been faxed to the hospital and a nurse was on the phone asking a specialist surgeon to come into the hospital as William was being prepared for the operating theatre.

William woke, three days later, hooked up to all kinds of tubes and machines and Officer Stead had visited in his free time to check on him. He saw that William was conscious and went into his room.

"Hey Stead, what's up?"

"How are you feeling Mad Dog? That was some crazy shit you put us through."

"I thought your life needed a bit of excitement."

"That was not excitement you crazy idiot. I really thought that was it, I thought you were dying."

William was thoughtful for a moment.

"I was dying. I could feel myself being pulled and I was resisting. I remember feeling that I could let go, it would be easy to go where I was being pulled."

He stopped talking and thought for a few seconds.

Stead leant forward in his armchair waiting for William to
continue.

"Then I heard this faraway voice shouting at me, telling me if I
try to escape I'll be shot dead," said William staring straight at
Officer Stead.

"Ha, I knew you could hear me. Huntley told me you couldn't
hear anything, and I told her that you could!"

"I couldn't tell it was your voice, just faint words coming from
faraway, but it was like being told there is a way back. It was crazy,
I can't explain the feelings or where I was. I felt like I was between.
Then those words pulled me back."

"Glad I could help."

"You saved me boss, you saved me. Give me a hug," William
said as he flung his arms out dramatically.

"Fuck off Mad Dog, you crazy bastard."

They were both laughing when the doctor came in the room.

"I see you are awake and functioning normally. How are you
feeling?" said the doctor as he checked the medical charts.

"Better than when I came here. I'm not dead, so that's a big
bonus. I've not felt sick in the past thirty minutes I've been awake.
How long was I out?

The doctor looked at Stead.

"I haven't had chance to tell him anything, we've been talking about how I saved him from going to the other side."

"I'm not convinced you've done me a favour, Stead. I'm going to have to go back to prison, unless you know otherwise?"

"TDCJ would have fired me if I'd let you die Mad Dog and I get good benefits with this job. I wasn't going to let you ruin that for me. They insist you come back to do more time."

William and Stead laughed whilst the doctor looked perturbed, unsure how to respond.

"Ok Doc, give him the run down."

"William, because your liver function is low, it's not able to handle all the waste it needs to process. As a result you were bleeding profusely from the veins in your oesophagus. All that blood was going into your stomach cavity and that was why you were vomiting blood all the time. Mr Stead got you here in the nick of time, a few more minutes and we couldn't have saved you. We had to tie the veins off with rubber bands to stop them bleeding. Don't worry they will dissolve in time when they've done their job."

"Thanks Doc, I really appreciate what you've done."

The doctor smiled in acknowledgement.

"I'm not sure how grateful I am that you've fixed me up to go back to that fucking prison where they are actively trying to kill me off."

The Doctor looked horrified.

"Don't worry Doc, only messing with you. They've been trying to kill me for years."

The doctor was unused to the prison banter and decided a stoic approach was best so continued dispensing his advice. "Stay away from alcohol and drugs, that can cause a relapse. Your liver needs a chance to recover, which it will if you give it a chance. We'll keep you here another forty eight to seventy two hours to monitor you, then you should be fit enough to leave."

William was returned to the prison, put in the hospice care unit for twenty one days until his weight was back up to a hundred and eighty pounds, and then released back to general population.

"Hey Mad Dog, you're back. Fuck me you look terrible," said Lenny who was seated eating a bowl of rice and chilli. He called up to three row as he continued, "Come and have something to eat. Hey Angel, bring a bowl for Mad Dog."

Angel left his house and peered over the railing. "Fuck me Mad Dog, we thought you were dead. The three of us packed up your shit to make sure nothing was stolen."

Mad Dog sat at the table eating and telling anyone who came to listen what had happened.

"Let's have a party later when Rat returns from work. He'll bring food back and we went to store yesterday. Lenny, go and get shit out of my locker to make a cheesecake," said Angel.

We'll leave the wine where it is for now," said Lenny.

"I'm glad you're ok Mad Dog."

William turned round to look at his cellie. Spider had transformed his personality since his near death experience of being dangled from three row. He was now quiet and respectful, taken up a vocation class to learn a trade and, a shock to the old inmates he had bullied, he apologised to them. He shared his food with them by way of making amends.

William had seen the change over a matter of months after Spider ceased being angry about his humiliation, putting his inflated ego aside. He accepted William's suggestion of enrolling in classes, educating himself. William had introduced him to Teacher to help guide Spider. Though William had never applied it to himself, he encouraged Spider to take any opportunity he could to better himself. Spider hadn't opened up to William on a personal level; that rarely happened in prison as it could be used against you to harm, threaten or extort. Spider discovered that, if he was straight with William, they could be friends, looking out for each other. William was Spider's secret role model.

"Hey Spider, come and sit down. What do you have in the locker to contribute to my welcome back party? How are classes going?"

"Am I invited to join you?"

"What are you talking about Spider, yes you're invited. We're cellies aren't we?"

Spider smiled. He was elated As he said, "I'm really enjoying carpentry Mad Dog. I love working with different woods, creating and building stuff. The teacher says I'm good at it, a natural, that's what he told me. I made something for you. I'll have to go and get it, though."

"Well, would you ever thought the Spider we were going to drop off three row would have turned into this Spider?" William said to Lenny and Angel.

"He's been a fucking pain in the ass the whole time you've been gone, asking us every fucking day if we heard anything about you," said Angel.

"He's been worried," said Lenny. "Can't imagine why he'd be worried about a worthless bastard like you."

"What can I say, he knows a real mother-fucker when he sees one. I think we've found a new addition to the team."

The party was in full flow and they had ten gallons of wine. One five gallon batch was harsher on the palate than the other, not fermenting as long. They'd sell the rubbish, whilst indulging uninhibited on the good batch. Lenny had retrieved a bag of wine from inside the vent at the top of his cell wall, and the other bag had been brought over by Rat, who had removed it from behind a vent in the wall of the laundry room, hidden amongst a cart full of inmate wash bags. These were nylon mesh bags, in which the inmate put their dirty clothes to be sent to the laundry. These bags were put in the washing machine and dryer, to be returned to the inmates the following day.

The guys had all drunk copious amounts of wine and different drugs were also available and consumed with abandon. William smoked only weed, having promised his Grandmother years ago that he wouldn't take Heroin again. He applied this to Cocaine plus other hard core drugs on offer. He didn't often smoke weed; it did nothing for him, except make him paranoid, so he tended to stay away from it. Clean of addiction, William didn't want to go down that road again, where his existence revolved around scoring his next fix, always seeking a bigger and better high. He'd spent years doing that and didn't miss it at all. Giving up heroin, he had gone cold turkey but hadn't had as hard a time of it as others he had seen go through it. It seemed that a lot was down to the state of mind; he'd decided to give it up and so he did just that. To William, it was as simplistic as that and he was happy to sell it to those who were still chasing that high and it was a lucrative hustle for him. The morality of his actions never concerned him; if they didn't buy it from him, they'd score from someone else.

The mood was good in the pod. One of Angel's guys had produced another five gallon bag of wine to contribute as quantities were running low. Many of the black inmates had been buying the wine so that they could participate. At a dollar fifty for a water bottle full, it was snapped up. Spider had taken charge of selling, filling up the bottles and taking payment. William glanced around, keeping his usual close eye on everything that was happening. No matter that the day-room was generally good-natured for a change, he knew that the mood could change in an instant. He looked over to the black guy, Fuzzy, in charge of the unit for his gang. He was deep in discussion with his deputy and they looked around the room, their eyes briefly resting on William. They turned away when they saw William had spotted them. William's mind went onto instant alert; something was off with them. He walked over to Angel and whispered in his ear, then told Lenny and Rat the same thing.

"Give me some wine," said a wiry black youngster with a surly tone. His nickname was Zoom, for his penchant for stealing luxury cars and then joyriding."

Spider filled his bottle and passed it back.

"Please is not a dirty word and neither is thank you. Hey, you haven't paid."

Zoom ignored him and Spider followed him. He was about to confront Zoom when Fuzzy and his deputy stepped in front of him. They both pushed Spider backwards at the same time. He stumbled and fell back into a group of black inmates who turned round in fury at being touched. They looked down at Spider trying to pull himself up from the floor, and the first one stuck his boot in Spider's ribcage.

"Set up," said William towards his group, his voice raised.

Everyone at the party stopped and turned to see what William was shouting about.

"Angel, this is it, the war is starting," said William. "We need Spider out of there."

Angel turned to his guys and pointed in the direction of the black gang soldiers kicking and stomping Spider who had no chance of escaping on his own.

"Get him out."

Twelve allies of Angel launched themselves into the Spider melee, punching, elbowing and kicking any black body that was in their way, ensuring that they would be out of action.

As soon as William's call to arms was uttered, Fuzzy screamed at his soldiers to fight.

"Kill as many as you can."

William followed the Mexicans, aiming to reach Spider as soon as they cleared a way for him to be dragged out but it wasn't happening. Two black gangsters were standing and jumping on Spider, punching and kicking out at the Mexicans at the same time. Spider's head was stomped repeatedly and William could see blood seeping from Spider's mouth. Spider opened his eyes and saw William and smiled at him, knowing that William was trying to save him. His free arm stretched out towards William.

"Hang on Spider, I'm getting you out."

Spider didn't hear what was said as one final stomp crushed his skull and William watched the life evaporate from Spider's body. William was filled with rage and stared at the black face of the man who had crushed in Spider's skull. The man was grinning maniacally as William reached into his pocket as he rushed towards the stomper. He pulled out a lethal looking shank. It didn't just look lethal, it was lethal. He had paid handsomely to have it made in the metal factory where they made toilets for the TDCJ units.

He stabbed furiously at the back of a black body in his path, pushing his blade up through his ribcage until all six inches of it reached the assailant's lung. He pulled the weapon out before the guy sagged to the floor. William lunged forward as his intended victim launched himself onto William. He couldn't see a weapon in the guy's hand so he allowed the guy through, not enough to knock William over, but enough that his opponent's momentum would drive the blade of his knife far into his body. It thrust into his muscle hardened stomach and the assailant gave a gut wrenching scream as he felt the pain of the blade as it cut him wide open. William pushed the guy sideways to land on the floor and pulled out the blade. He sliced it across the side of his neck, cutting the jugular vein. He knew Opponent was finished when the artery spurted blood unrestricted.

William stepped back and looked around for Fuzzy who was being taken care of by Lenny who had jumped on his back. Lenny had Fuzzy's head in a vice lock and, using his own home-made shank, thrust it first into his temple, then into his neck, stabbing in a frenzy. Even as Fuzzy went down, Lenny clung on, still impaling his opponent. He stopped when Angel and Rat pulled him away.

The fighting was bloody and brutal with everyone in the pod involved. There wasn't a choice, it was a fight for your own race. If you failed to retaliate you were dealt with brutally as a race traitor. The fighting raged for two hours before enough officers were found to tackle it and, by this time, the 'war' had spread throughout the unit. Inmates were fighting in every section, pod and building and those inmates outside on recreation time also fought.

The officer in the picket had repeatedly shouted for the inmates to lie on the ground or he would shoot but his words fell on deaf ears. He had called Captain Mauser for instructions on how to proceed.

Do nothing until we get teams there, he had been instructed.

Two things happened in close succession: first, several Army vehicles arrived carrying dozens of soldiers. They filed in an orderly fashion through the door into the unit to take instructions for quelling the fighting. A dozen fully armed soldiers were sent to each building to take back control. Second, two Black Ops military helicopters came over the horizon and each hovered low over the recreation yard.

A commanding voice blared over a tannoy coming from the air.

"Stop fighting and lie on the ground. We are armed with live rounds and will kill you if we have to fire."

Most of the inmates stopped fighting at the threat of death and dropped to the ground, some lying , some sitting. Most were nursing wounds of some sort. The soldiers inside the building were equally as successful. They ran into one pod after another, issuing the same warning as had come from the helicopter and the inmates dropped to the ground. The concrete looked like it had received a poor paint job, with swathes of crimson blood covering large areas.

The soldiers waited, weapons at the ready, until each inmate had been secured with plasticuffs and pushed onto the floor against the day room wall.

Two nurses with a gurney came in to remove Spider's body and William looked grim.

"Those mother-fuckers are going to pay for killing Spider," he said, addressing Angel, "The kid was turning his life around, he didn't deserve that."

He looked over to one of the inmates who had stomped on Spider and they made eye contact. The guy smirked as William made a slicing motion across his throat and pointed at him.

A full on investigation began immediately with free-world homicide detectives and TDCJ Internal Affairs (free world police working inside the prison) involved. It took weeks to finish the investigation and the whole unit, plus several other units in the state, stayed locked down for the duration with only essential movement was allowed.

After forty eight hours, perceived instigators and the most disruptive inmates considered were shipped to units across the state. Scores of others were placed in disciplinary segregation until the investigation was finished. The atmosphere throughout the unit was subdued.

There were regular cell searches during this time. This caused animosity from the inmates towards the officers, especially as officers were often careless with the meagre possessions of inmates. It mattered not one iota to officialdom that families paid exorbitantly for the few things allowed, such as radios, fans, typewriters, hot-pots, food, photographs, and even clothing. All inmates in the Texas prison system were required to work but were not paid for the labour they performed. Hustling, stealing and borrowing was how trade worked in prison, which exacerbated existing problems. For some officers, cell searches were a way to exert and parade their power, choosing to forgo a standard cell search, instead 'tossing' the cell. This would involve throwing the contents of inmate's storage boxes across the floor, ripping electrical items from the wall sockets, throwing them out on the run and laughing when they heard something break.

Officer Roscoe was back to work and the section of ear Blaine had bitten off was never found. Roscoe appeared deformed, his head off-kilter, with most of one ear missing and was holding a bigger grudge than usual. His mission was to make the white boys lives more miserable than they were already; revenge was his plan and every white boy would pay a high price.

William was seated at the table talking to Teacher, Thumper - Teacher's new cellie - and Rat when Roscoe came on the pod. He looked around the day-room as he strode towards the door of a cell, then motioned to the picket officer to open the electronic door and instructed the two black inmates who had been sleeping to leave. Roscoe performed a cursory search, lifting the mattresses, checking for holes or repairs that would indicate tampering for the purpose of hiding contraband. He opened locker doors to inspect what was inside. He looked up at the vents, seeking evidence of their removal, another common cache. He found nothing so allowed the occupants back inside.

"Well we know who the snitches are don't we," said William in disgust.

"There are more snitches than there are decent mother-fucker convicts on this farm," said Rat.

Roscoe looked over to William's table then turned back to the occupants of the cell. He spoke a few words to them and pointed over to the group. When he was finished with his questions he gave them a gang hand signal.

Roscoe strutted over to William's team's table and asked about the cells where they lived, giving Rat a long lingering look, remembering the altercation which resulted in the loss of half his ear. He put his hand up to his ear and Rat smirked.

"You," he said to William, "Which is your house?"

William told him and Roscoe went to the cell, again indicating to the picket officer to roll the door. William stayed put as Roscoe pulled up his mattress and pulled out William's clean clothes that were lying underneath. They fell on the floor as Roscoe wandered over to William's locker and pulled out everything inside. Pathetically, he made a point of standing on packets of tortilla chips and bags of rice, until the bags burst open and spilled their contents over the floor. He ripped open a packet of tortilla chips on the pretext of checking for drugs and emptied a bag of coffee to inspect the bottom of the packet. Finally, Roscoe picked up a bottle of lotion, inspected its base and squeezed the contents over William's strewn property. Then he threw it down into the mess.

"What the fuck, you fucking punk-ass mother-fucking bitch," snarled an infuriated William.

"Get this shit cleaned up," said Roscoe. "Just because you're in prison doesn't mean you have to live like a pig, White Boy."

William had his fists bunched up ready to attack Roscoe. He had paid Rat to bring him a new set of clothes and Roscoe had just ruined them and destroyed at least twenty dollars worth of commissary at the same time. Roscoe had no idea how lucky he was as William decided to forgo attacking him for it would undoubtedly have ended with Roscoe at best in the hospital, and William doing a long stretch in disciplinary segregation.

At least he didn't find my stash in the false back of my locker.

Rat had a bad feeling; he knew he was in for worse than William had received. Roscoe looked at him with narrowed eyes and a grin full of bad intent.

"You white boy, which is your house? I'm looking forward to this."

Rat bounded up the stairs with Thumper close behind him and Roscoe lumbered after them, puffing and panting by the time he reached the cell. He pushed Rat aside and took little notice of the stream of vitriol that came from Rat's mouth. After the picket officer opened the door he entered the cell, leaving a trail of devastation. He did the same things that he'd done in William's cell, grinding the mess into Rat and Thumper's sheets, clothes and paperwork. He picked up a large manila envelope, bursting at the seams with papers, Thumper's legal paperwork, a copy of his trial transcript and his appeal, which had just been denied. He spent a moment flicking through it, knowing that it was illegal to read an inmate's legal correspondence but Roscoe didn't care. He would do exactly what he wanted to do. If the white boys didn't like it, tough, they should have stayed out of prison.

"Hey mother-fucker, keep your fucking filthy ape hands off my legal paperwork," Thumper shouted at him.

"Or what?" Roscoe said as he stepped out of the cell and stood nose to nose with Thumper.

"Or I'll beat your bitch-ass to a pulp."

Roscoe smirked as he turned to go back in the cell. He peered up at the shelf above the toilet.

"Two typewriters," he said with evident joy, "Someone has money."

"Touch those and you're a dead man," said Rat.

"Oh yeah," Roscoe said, glancing at the insignificant appearance of Rat, continuing with, "You think you can take me on do you snowflake?"

Before Rat could respond, Roscoe picked up one of the typewriters and threw it down on the floor with enough force that it broke apart. It was certainly of no further use. Thumper and Rat were having a whispered debate about how to handle Roscoe when they saw the second typewriter come sliding across the floor out of the cell. It hit the metal railing support which caused it to shatter with pieces dropping into the day room below. The rest of it littered the run. Roscoe strolled out of the cell grinning.

"All finished. Get that shit cleaned up."

"Fuck you asshole," said Rat as he walked towards his door.

Roscoe turned his back on the guys and that was the moment Thumper struck. There was no thought or strategy behind it, just pent up frustration and hate-filled aggression. His sister had bought him the typewriter to work on his appeal and he would need one to work on his case further, at a cost of almost two hundred dollars. He took a running jump onto Roscoe's back and clung on with one of his forearms around Roscoe's head, the other hand pulling the prison issue razor out of his trouser pocket. As Roscoe tried to shake Thumper off him, Thumper, in a state of rage sliced the impeccably sharpened serrated blade across the front of Roscoe's neck. He sliced straight across the front of his throat, his own arm impeding a lengthier cut. In a fit of savagery Thumper used the blade prolifically to cut open Roscoe's face. He made sure that the new look was as terrible as his personality. He jumped down as Roscoe fell to the floor screaming. Thumper knew his next stop was solitary confinement so he went into his cell calmly to pack up the rest of his possessions.

After medical staff had taken Roscoe away and sent him to the hospital, half a dozen officers came on the pod and finished the cell searches. Whilst not causing the same amount of damage as Roscoe, they made little effort to be respectful. Their contraband findings were meagre as there had been time between Roscoe's fiasco and the new officers coming in to hide what was there.

46

William was in medical having his blood-work done again and was locked in the office with Nurse Carling. They had indulged in sex and now William was eating a burger and fries she had brought in for him. She had also brought him a beer poured into a drinks cup from the burger restaurant. William had already hidden the drugs about his person. There was a knock at the door which made the nurse jump. William laughed.

"We've been busted."

Nurse Carling gave him a withering look and opened the door to see an angry looking sergeant. He gave Nurse Carling a look of disgust as he saw William in her office finishing his meal and looked William up and down. William smirked at him as he popped the last few fries into his mouth.

"I see you have yourself a new plaything," the sergeant said to Nurse Carling.

"Fuck you Pablo."

"You seem to forget you're my wife."

"Biggest mistake of my life."

"You, inmate, stay away from my wife and keep your hands to yourself, or else," said the Sergeant.

"Or fucking what Sergeant Alvarez?" William said, emphasising the sergeant's name as he made a point of reading the name badge.

"Or I'll make your life hell."

William laughed as he said,. "In case you hadn't realised asshole, it already is hell. It's a supermax prison, designed to be hell."

"Leave him alone," said Nurse Carling.

"Like I told you inmate, stay away from my wife or you'll be reading about it."

William stood up as he said, "If you think I give a fuck about a case you are fucking crazy. I've got a seventy five year sentence. What the fuck do you think you can do to me, asshole?"

William laughed as he left Nurse Carling's office.

"That's a funny husband you have Dracula. See you next time."

William was stretched out on his bunk, reading, when newly promoted Sergeant Donovan came by to give William the paper work for a disciplinary case.

"Sorry Mad Dog, I couldn't pull it and get rid of it. I was off for a couple of days and didn't see it in time."

"What is it?"

Sergeant Alvarez has written out a major case saying you assaulted Nurse Carling in medical.

"Well that's bullshit. I've never laid my hands on a woman, and I'd beat the shit out of any man who did."

"Ok, calm down. I'm on my way over for a statement from Nurse Carling but I wanted you to know I'm doing the investigation. I'll come back to you in a while."

"That fucking Alvarez needs killing," said William to Angel as he left the cell to join Angel at the table. William told him what had happened and the case that Sergeant Alvarez had filed.

"There's too much shit going on here right now," said Angel. "It's getting out of control. I don't know about you, but I've had my cell tossed seven times in the last couple of days."

"Yeah I know, mine's been done six times. Those mother-fuckers left me no bags of chips, rice or oatmeal. I'd only just been to commissary and they threw most of it away. I nearly popped one of them in the mouth when he dropped and stood on my pint of ice-cream. Fucking assholes."

"Rat has had it even worse. They were in his house again now, four times today that I've seen. He put a grievance in about his typewriter but the answer came back as the usual - nothing to do with them. He's written to the warden."

"Oh here we go," said William as he spotted Sergeant Alvarez walk in the door. "This is trouble come to visit."

Sergeant Alvarez headed straight to William's cell and waited for the picket officer to open before stepping inside. He bent down and opened William's locker, reaching in to the back and sweeping everything out onto the floor. He then stomped on everything and ground his heels in, causing maximum damage. Then he pulled out William's storage box from under his bunk, opened it out and pulled paperwork out, throwing it everywhere. William was raging.

"Get out of my fucking cell, you fucking deranged mother-fucker."

Sergeant Alvarez squared up to William even though he was a good foot shorter and screamed back in William's face.

"Get out of my face you fucking nurse beater."

Back and forth the abuse and insults were hurled.

"Get the fucking LT here now," William shouted at nobody in particular. As they hurled more barbs at each other, the officer in the picket called for a lieutenant to come to the section.

Out of the corner of his eye William saw both Captain Hauser and Sergeant Wood walk in the door as Alvarez was screaming in his face. William took a step backwards a smile forming on his mouth. This seemed to tip Alvarez over the edge and he lost control, taking a swing at William. His fist connected with William's chin. While surprised at the ferocity of the punch, it wasn't entirely unexpected. William had been increasing his taunts of Alvarez and his status as a man. The timing of the slug couldn't have been any better and William felt his bottom front teeth dislodge. He didn't have time to give that any thought before he received a punch to one temple and another to his other. William was going to have two very black eyes but he sat on his bunk to avoid retaliating; no need now for Alvarez had been caught red handed assaulting him.

"Sergeant Alvarez," shouted Captain Hauser, "Step out of the cell now."

"Come on mother-fucker, aren't you going to fight back?" Alvarez taunted, ignoring Captain Hauser's command.

"Sergeant Alvarez, step out of the cell now," Captain Hauser ordered from the doorway.

Sergeant Alvarez turned to see who was calling his name. Pumped up with adrenaline, he wasn't going to tolerate an inmate challenging him. Still having clenched fists, ready to fight, it took him a moment to recognise the captain. As recognition hit his brain, he dropped his fists.

"What do you think you are doing?"

"I was doing a cell search, and this inmate attacked me."

"Why were you doing cell searches, and why this cell? There were no searches on the rota for this building today."

"I was told he had drugs."

"Bullshit," said William.

"Mad Dog, calm down," said Captain Hauser. "Put in a grievance about this, and I'll see you are given compensation for your commissary items."

"That's fucking bullshit Captain, and you know it. How am I going to be compensated for my damaged and destroyed legal paperwork, photographs and magazines?"

"Nothing I can do about that Mad Dog," Captain Hauser said as he took Sergeant Alvarez by the arm and guided him away from the cells.

"Straight to my office Sergeant. We have some things to talk about. Sergeant Wood, take Mad Dog to store. He needs to replace all his commissary items."

Captain Hauser explained to Sergeant Alvarez that he would be demoted for his assault on William and Alvarez was humiliated and furious about being admonished for doing his job. He'd let his temper run away from him but William deserved what he received for having an inappropriate relationship with his wife. Was he supposed to just ignore it?

"Come in," called Captain Hauser in response to the knock at his door and looked up to see Sergeant Donovan enter.

"I've done the investigation on the case Sergeant Alvarez filed against Mad Dog. Nurse Carling, who happens to be Sergeant Alvarez's wife, has denied that she was assaulted by Mad Dog or anyone else. She is prepared to take a lie detector test, if asked."

"She's lying," said Alvarez. "She's protecting the inmate. I checked his file, you know he has over two hundred on record assaults on officers whilst restrained."

"According to the case you wrote, you saw Mad Dog hit and push Nurse Carling. You wrote that she screamed as she fell over and bashed her knee as she fell to the floor." Sergeant Donovan said.

"That's what happened, I saw him do it."

"Nurse Carling agreed to be checked over by the provider and another nurse. There were no recent marks, bruises or injuries on her. No one heard her scream and she maintains that the inmate in question has not laid a finger on her or been disrespectful in any way. On what grounds have you written this case?"

"He deserves it," said Alvarez.

"That isn't a reason Alvarez. You know it's a federal offence to falsify official state documents. I've no choice but to put you on suspension until you see the warden. I'm sorry." Captain Hauser said.

"So that's it, he gets away with it, and I'm going to get fired?" Alvarez said, his temper flaring again.

"That's for the warden to decide," said Captain Hauser.

Two days later Alvarez stood in front of the warden.

"There is no justification for such levels of behaviour," said Warden Smith. "I may be fighting a losing battle, but I'll be damned if I let corruption and abuse of power go on when I know about it. I have no other choice but to let you go."

"So that's it, you are taking the inmate's side?" Alvarez said.

It's not about taking the inmate's side but about your wrongdoing against an inmate and the system. You can't decide to target an inmate you don't like and then fabricate offences."

"They are fucking criminals, who cares?"

"I care. Now, Sergeants Donovan and Wood will go with you to collect your belongings and you'll be escorted off state property immediately. Good luck."

41

"It's fucking ridiculous," said Rat after yet another cell search. He was moaning to anyone who would listen. Some inmates on the pod being targeted and, although officially it was the Warden trying to clean up the unit, there was clearly retaliation happening for the attack on Roscoe. Nobody knew what happened to him; officers weren't talking or they didn't know. That revenge was being taken was obvious to everyone. Those being targeted were friends of Blaine and Rat. William came over to the table where Lenny was seated.

"Fucking assholes," said William to the four officers who had come on the pod.

The same four had arrived every day of the four day shifts they worked and it had been going on for a while. Whether they were on first, second or third shift didn't matter. A shift in the middle of the night gave officers a bigger advantage; the inmates were asleep.

"You, seven bottom, get your ass out here now," said Officer Burton after pulling a cell number out of a hat. Burton was a short black man, self conscious about his size, compensating by taking up boxing as a teenager. He felt a compunction to fight anyone willing to take him on, plus many others who weren't willing, as a way to validate himself. It served to give him a bad attitude and he did his utmost to humiliate anyone who faced him.

Officers Flaherty, Torres and Robinson stood a couple of steps behind Burton, each wearing sturdy boots. Torres, short and squat, of Italian descent, wore leather gloves. Both Flaherty, who had Irish heritage, and Robinson, family from an unknown African country, were both six feet tall, neither large nor muscular, but certainly not skinny. Flaherty, who had numerous brothers and sisters, came from a background where bare-knuckle fighting was popular and was a savage fighter. Robinson hated inmates so was willing to inflict any damage on them that he could achieve without being disciplined. Torres had spent most of his childhood in trouble and was a dirty fighter. A motley crew.

William heard his door unlock. He was predisposed to fighting but this 'game' the officers were now playing was something else.

They knew what they were doing was immoral, an abuse of power and illegal but didn't care because rank, or enough of them, knew what they were doing. Collusion was essential or it could not continue.

William stepped from his cell ready for an unfair fight and knew that he was going down and allow it unless he exacted some damage himself. He wore the boots he'd purchased from commissary, not the best quality, but better than him wearing his shower slides. William also wore shorts to provide freedom of movement, not possible with prison issue trousers, three sizes too big. He came out slowly, appearing reluctant. The officers didn't move as William came tentatively closer. When he was two steps away from Burton, William sprang to life, jumping forward, swinging his fist hard into the side of Burton's head. The Officer dropped to his knees as the shock of the impact hit him, dazed with stars twinkling in front of his eyes. Flaherty, Torres and Robinson were momentarily startled but, as they saw Burton drop, sprang to life. They launched themselves on William, who put up a good fight, spurred on by the shouts of encouragement coming from the cells. William managed to knee Torres in the groin, elbow Robinson in his chest and landed a lucky punch, splatting Flaherty's nose all over his face. The Officers soon dropped him though and all William could do to protect himself was curl up into a ball covering his face and protecting his groin. The officers took full advantage of his exposed torso and legs with kicks and stomps continuing for what felt like hours, in reality minutes. They stopped as they became tired and Burton had recovered by then. He stood, looking down at William, said nothing, instead raining a barrage of brutal kicks at William. Burton was about to turn away when he decided on one last assault. He turned back and stomped with as much force as he could muster on William's head and only William's arms covering his face stopped his head from bouncing on the concrete.

"Get up mother-fucker. We need to take you to medical to get checked out and make sure the fight you've just had with another inmate hasn't damaged you." Burton said as the other officers sniggered at this comment.

Robinson and Flaherty took one arm of William's each and hauled him up. They kept hold of his arms to help William walk, but they hadn't reached the door before Flaherty tripped William, repeating the ruse as they walked along the concrete side-walk to one building where medical was housed. As Flaherty tripped him the second time, William dropped face first as Flaherty and Robinson let him go. His nose smacked on the concrete, leaving an explosion of blood over himself and the grey paving. Flaherty gave him a swift kick in his ribs, then they pulled him upright again as Torres laughed at his 'clumsiness'.

"Fuck you assholes," said William as he spat blood out of his mouth.

"What the fuck," said Nurse Carling as she emerged from her office having heard William's voice. "Not you as well? I have seen so many inmates in here with bootprints etched on their bodies that I have been taking photographs. What the fuck is going on?"

William told her about the raid and that officers had been taking retaliatory measures. Nurse Carling was used to hearing wild stories from inmates, often so that they could come to medical and eye up the female staff, even masturbate in front of them. She knew that William had no reason to lie to her. Besides, the broken nose, cuts and bruises and the boot imprints confirmed what he had told her. She told William to strip down to his shorts as she retrieved the camera from her desk drawer. She photographed him from many angles, making sure that she had evidence of each mark on him, keeping the zoom function on for injuries on his numerous tattoos.

"I've been suspicious for a while," she said, "I started taking photographs and writing reports on each inmate when they were brought in and noticed that it was always the same officers who brought them here. What do you think I should do about it?"

"I'll tell you what you do," William said as he dressed, "Get them to Angel's mother. She came to visit yesterday and saw the condition of him and is creating holy hell. Get her phone number from his file, in fact, do it now and call her, I know her well so she will listen when I tell her to work with you on this."

Nurse Carling spent a couple of minutes tapping away on her computer until she found the required information. She picked up the phone and dialled the number. It took several rings before Angel's mother answered and, when she did, a suspicious tone to her voice.

"Hey Maria, it's Mad Dog."

"Mad Dog, what the hell? What the fuck is going on? I saw Angel yesterday beaten almost to a pulp. He told me what's happening and I've called everyone from the Ombudsman to the Governor and our attorney. Of course the Ombudsman is useless, haven't had a response from that worthless bitch of a governor and my attorney says we need some proof. I am fucking raging mad."

"Here's what you need to do Maria," William said, before she could draw breath and start talking again," Nurse Carling, here, has been collating evidence, taking photos and writing her own reports. She hasn't done anything with them yet because she doesn't know who she can trust to deal with it. I want you to meet up with her somewhere and get the reports and photos. Let me give you her phone number. Dracula, what's your home phone number?"

He closed the call by telling them to avoid making arrangements over any phone on the unit, but suggested they meet soon.

"Mad Dog, I've a good mind to send my boys after those mother-fuckers," Maria told him.

"Well hold off. You can do that if it doesn't get resolved the way we want."

William rang off and Nurse Carling saw him wince as he sat down in the chair.

"Ok, drop your pants, I'll give you a painkiller injection and order a weeks supply. There'll be a pill at the window in a couple of days. Here's enough to last you until then," she said as she handed him a card of tablets as he pulled up his pants.

When William returned to the day room, he called the guys over to explain what had been discussed.

"Angel, Dracula is going to get together with your mother and give her a copy of all the photographs and personal reports she's written on all the guys she has seen the last couple of weeks with boot prints on them."

"You know what she's like Mad Dog, if anyone can get things sorted she can."

"She's like a pit-bull on a cat's ass"

Everyone laughed at his description, which temporarily served to lighten their mood.

"I've some wine ready," said Lenny, "Why don't we have ourselves a little pity party?"

"Great idea," said Rat, "I've a pass to go to commissary. What does everyone want?"

"I'm going to make a chocolate cheesecake," said William as Rat left, with a list of requests.

Teacher returned from commissary with Rat, both carrying bags stuffed with goodies.

"Fuck me Teach, your face isn't looking any better yet," said William as he studied Teacher's visage. He had been the chosen victim on the rogue officers' previous four day shift. His cheek was swollen from a fractured cheekbone, eye clamped shut from the swelling, and there were still the marks from the boot print that had been ground into his face.

"I'm losing weight because I can't eat properly," he said through puffy lips. "I can't drink very well either, but you can be fucking sure it won't stop me getting drunk."

"You boys all look terrible," said Charlie as he arrived back at the day-room after a day spent in the law library. He spent everyday there as he had three cases on the go against TDCJ. Consequently, he had missed out on the beatings although, the one time his bunk number had been called, the rogue four saw who he was and chose an alternative cell.

42

"What the hell has happened to you Mad Dog?" Sergeant Donovan said as he handed William three baggies of weed.

"Fucking rogue c.o.'s," he said. William explained again what had been happening.

"Can I help?"

"Get copies from Nurse Carling of the evidence she has then contact ACLU, the American Civil Liberties Union, about what's going on. Give them copies of the photos and reports she's has written. Hopefully they will take on the case."

"Right, I'll go over and see her now. I've heard talk of what's been going on but didn't believe it, it seemed too far-fetched. I didn't believe officers would do that sort of thing."

"Donovan, there is more corruption inside of prisons than there is in politics."

"I'm starting to see that."

"It's not the first time I've seen it happen or been part of it," William said, "Contacting the ACLU was the only reason it was stopped last time."

Donovan walked straight to the infirmary, spoke to Nurse Carling about what Mad Dog had told him.

The same four officers came on the pod four days later and stood in the middle of the day room, making a drama from pulling a piece of paper out of Torres' baseball cap.

"Six bottom," one of them called out, looking in the direction of cell number six. Old man Lang was seventy five years old, recovering from a heart attack. He hobbled out of his cell using a walking frame and the officers laughed.

"Come out swinging old timer or your time's up," Officer Flaherty said.

Offender Lang was unsteady on his feet despite the use of his walker and, as soon as he stepped from the cell, he dropped to his knees in surrender. The officers laughed raucously, ignoring the fear in his eyes. Lang knew that he wasn't going to survive the onslaught and scanned around desperately for someone to help him but everyone was locked in their cells. He locked eyes with William who, like every other inmate, was up against the window of their door, watching everything.

"Mad Dog," he said, his voice betraying his weakness, "Take care of my stuff and let my son know what has happened."

William nodded to assure the old man that he would do as requested. He was upset about the old man, had done time with him in several different prisons and Lang had looked out for William when he was a youngster in the system. He was also his source for moving cash from the unit. William joined the chorus of voices screaming abuse, insults and threats at the officers as Burton kicked away the walking frame and they launched kicks on Lang. As he lay on the floor, dying, he no longer felt the brutal kicks to his body, or the vicious stomps on his head and limbs which broke his bones.

The inmates fell silent as the officers stepped back to survey their work. Criminals though they were, each of them was sickened at the brutal murder of a defenceless old man. They started up the shouting again as the officers picked up the broken floppy limbs of the old man, letting them fall again for their sadistic entertainment. They laughed as they half carried and dragged Lang inside of his cell.

"How are we going to explain his broken bones?" asked Robinson. He could see suspicions being raised.

"We'll say we found him like that, his cellie beat him. Who are they going to believe? Us or a bunch of criminals?" said Flaherty, "They'll have sent the body to the morgue before bruises appear, so there will be no need for an autopsy."

The other three nodded at Flaherty's apparent wisdom of this until Robinson said, "Do bruises develop when someone is dead?"

They all thought for a moment.

"No idea," said Burton, "He'll be gone by then, so it doesn't matter."

"Hey Mad Dog," said Donovan when they met up in an unused room a few weeks later. He had called William over to present an update for him, "ACLU were all over the case like a rash on a leper. I took the info Nurse Carling gave me to Captain Hauser. I knew I could trust him and we met with someone from ACLU, not wanting to leave it to email. They've started an investigation with the state police and OIG immediately."

"That's good. Those mother-fuckers have turned up the heat, particularly on Angel. You can't tell what he's supposed to look like any more," William said, "He went to visit his mother at the weekend and she told him that the cops have been on her doorstep everyday to harass her. It turns out Burton has a brother who is a cop and he is getting in on the action."

"I will pass that tit-bit onto ACLU too," Donovan said, "I'm not supposed to tell you this, but they are planting a guy as part of the investigation. Angel will be getting a new cellie."

"Now, that is interesting because he got a new cellie last night."

"I'm fucking sick of all this shit," said Rat, as he returned from medical after another beating from the four rogue officers. "I'm not going to fucking spend the next twenty years or more putting up with this. We need to do something about it. I think we need a plan of action."

"What sort of plan," said Angel through the side of his swollen mouth.

"Well I'm ready to take myself out of the game. Fuck this shit, fuck these bitch-ass corrupt officers, fuck prison. Look at us, we're too beaten up to fight. I think we make it big."

"Big, how?" William said, his interest piqued.

"We plan it out when and how we will die. I think murder by cop would be good," said Rat.

"Are you fucking crazy?" Lenny said, "How are we supposed to do that?"

"That's going to take time to plan out," said Teacher.

"Time is what we all have plenty of, " said William. "Except you Teach, you'll be going home in a couple of years, getting your life back."

"I can still help you plan," Teacher said.

"So how do we go about planning it?" said Lenny.

"I just got moved into maintenance to work," said Rat. "I have access to the blueprints of the whole unit. That's what got me thinking."

"Can you make a copy of the blueprints?" William said.

"I think so, let me see tonight at work."

"Otherwise you'll have to draw it all out on paper for us," William said.

"How are we going to get enough guns to finish ourselves off," said Lenny.

"The idea is to be killed by the law, you fucking idiot," said Angel. "Otherwise we could do it ourselves, with a huge overdose. Where is the drama in that?"

"I have an idea forming but I need a copy of the blueprints to know if it's going to work," said William, deep in thought.

Rat came out of his cell the following day and joined the others at the table.

"I drew the whole fucking plan of the unit onto paper. The fucking copy machine in the maintenance office was broken. Like this whole fucking prison."

"Where is it now?" said William.

Rat took a furtive look around the day room to check that no one was taking any notice of them. He ensured that neither the rover officer was currently in the section or the desk officer was taking an interest in them. He rummaged around in the pocket of his over-sized white trousers; they didn't come with pockets but inmates add them.

After giving another glance around the room, Rat unfolded the A4 size piece of paper. It was some feat to fold it so small but Rat had plenty of practice over the years. The five of them bent over the table studying the drawings.

"This is good," said William, "I think my plan can work. We could do with three or four more guys to come in with us to make it easier."

"That's no problem," said Angel, "Two of my guys Carlos One and Carlos Two are all for it, they both have life without parole."

"Same for my work partner," said Lenny, "He has a ninety nine year sentence and he is sixty years old so he's not getting out. He's in the dorms but he will come out of place to be here."

"Good, we should manage with seven," said William.

"So what's the plan Mad Dog?" said Rat, making William the unelected leader.

Before William could explain, the rover officer came onto the section. He made a beeline for the table, curious to see why so many guys were grouped around something.

"Watch out Jigger about," said Teacher, using a prison slang term to alert inmates that an officer was present. He spotted the officer as he stopped by to speak to the desk officer.

William folded the paper and placed it in his own trouser pocket. Teacher put a couple of books he'd been carrying on top of the table to make it appear that they had been studying them.

"What are you mother-fuckers up to?" said Officer Arturo, pushing Rat aside to see was absorbed their attention.

"Hey, keep your bitch-ass hands off me if you want to walk out of here on your own," snarled Rat.

Officer Arturo smirked as he said, "I asked you fucking losers a question. What are you doing?"

"None of your fucking business. Get the fuck away from us, go and suck the major's dick, it's what you do best," Angel said

Angel had a hatred of Hispanic officers who made life hard for their own people; Arturo came into that category, coming down harder on his own people than he did others in the mistaken belief that it made him respected. It did the opposite, making him despised.

"Calm down Angel. I'd hate to break the news to your harassed mother that her precious boy had to be put in seg for threats to an officer. The way I hear it, she's busy enough with the cops on her doorstep everyday. You wouldn't want to upset her more would you?" Arturo said.

Angel took a menacing step towards the officer and, at the same time, Carlos One and Two both stepped forward from the wall that had been supporting them. They were ready to back up their leader and William could see the danger. He stepped in front of Angel to diffuse the situation.

"Either suck my dick or fuck off and crawl back in the gutter you share with those deranged mother-fuckers you are on shift with," he said.

The comment he'd made about cops and Angel's mother told William that Arturo was party to the actions of the rogue officers. He stored away the information. Arturo was another officer about to be brought down but that was for later.

"Ok girls, no need to get your panties in a knot," Arturo said as he stepped away and turned round to leave the table.

"Fucking race traitor asshole," said Angel to Arturo's back.

The guys watched Arturo leave the section and restarted their conversation about their plan.

"Ok, here's what I think will work," said William. "we do it on second shift because it's six females and only one male."

"If we make it this card, it means that male will be fucking Arturo," said Angel. "It's working for me so far."

Angel was still mad from the encounter and the others nodded in agreement.

"So we stage a little distraction fight whilst I take out the male desk officer, probably slit his throat will be quickest and easiest. Get his uniform off him and one of you guys will put it on. We then call for the rover officer, which will be Arturo, to come over and we take him out the same way. Someone then puts his uniform on. We do the same on each pod and in the picket until we have taken the whole building," said William.

"Are we killing the females?" said Lenny, uncomfortable at the thought.

"No. We handcuff them and lock in the unused room, behind the desk."

Everyone showed relief because it wasn't the done thing to kill a woman, a fundamental rule.

"Once we have control of the building, we take the two dead officers out to the rec yard so they will be visible. Then we call the administration and tell them we have control of the building."

William paused to take a drink of his tea.

"That's why the blueprints were useful," said Rat, "To confirm that the laws, when they come, can see the yard and the whole building. We need them to know that we've taken control."

"So then what happens?" Teacher said.

"Then the Warden calls in the Texas Rangers and they will be here faster than you can eat a soup!" said Angel.

"The Warden is bound to call us. He'll want to know what it is that we want. A The Warden will try to convince us to give it up peacefully and we will give them a list of ridiculous demands. They can't and won't give us anything, besides that isn't why we are doing this. We may as well have some fun with them," said Rat.

"We could ask for a helicopter to take us somewhere and a million dollars each," said Lenny.

The mood had become jovial and they joked about the ludicrous demands they would make.

"The Rangers will place snipers in the towers most definitely and, when we don't give it up, they will take us out of the game. Then it's over," said William, scanning the table.

"Fuck me," said Teacher, "No offence guys, but you have convinced me, doing my last couple of years, to keep my nose clean and be released to a new life. That's the way to go for me, that's what you told me."

"I'm happy to hear you say that Teach, you always had more to lose. None of us do. So, how about a time to set this in motion," said William.

Everyone had a different time-frame in mind, ranging from the following week, to a month's time.

"I would say, give it three months for things to improve. If they don't, we do it then," said William.

The plan was approved and agreed by each of the guys, with Rat approving it on behalf of Sailor Jack, his work partner.

44

"Someone sent me a Christmas card from overseas," said Angel, looking down at the return address of Ireland written on the envelope in his hand and, as he held the unopened envelope towards William, continued, "I don't have time to write to anyone overseas."

"I've got nothing but time," said William as he took the envelope and turned it over and over in his hands, but didn't open it. He smiled as he slid it into his shirt pocket.

Later, seated on his bunk, William ripped open the envelope. For some reason, he'd been experiencing a positive feeling all day and h read the card, which had a comical Father Christmas stuck halfway in a chimney on the front, and words inside wishing him a

Happy Christmas plus an explanation of why he was receiving the card. His name had been given as part of an inmate card swap. William was astounded that such a thing existed and that anyone, let alone someone from the other side of the world, would send cards to prisoners.

He was feeling warm vibes again as he read, then re-read, the card. He put it back in his pocket to keep it with him. He thought long and hard for several days on whether he would reply the sender. Was there any point? They had set their plan in motion, with two months left before it would be enacted. Finally, he decided that he would reply.

If she doesn't write back, the plan goes ahead. If she replies, then she is a keeper and the plan is over for me.

Christmas Day was when William wrote an eight page response. He wrote about how he'd been given the card by a friend, and was amazed that someone would take the time to do something so nice for a criminal. He described the jobs he'd done before he came to prison, explaining that he'd been married but was no longer and that she had never written nor visited him. He also told in the letter that his wife, despite promising to retain a lawyer for him, had sold the house he'd built, his possessions, pocketed their money and moved to a different state where she instigated divorce proceedings. He was honest about the crime that brought him to prison this time, making no excuses nor indulging in self pity. He finished the letter by saying that he was an animal lover and dealt harshly with anyone who abused or neglected them. He held onto the letter for a while before adding it to the prison mailbox, where it would remain for two days . He didn't want to give an officer the opportunity to throw the letter away.

On Christmas Day, the inmates were given a special meal for lunch: Turkey and ham, three different vegetables, for once not boiled to a mush, mashed and roast potatoes, stuffing, gravy, and two different deserts. Half pint cartons of both milk and orange juice were part of the meal. This was one of the few days that William went to the chow hall to eat and the guys sat at the same table, talking about the plan. They had already decided which shift would be working on the day, where they would take named officers hostage, how they would access weapons and what they would do to make sure that they were killed by other officers. William dropped a bombshell.

"I've written a letter to the woman who sent the Christmas card," he said. "If she writes back, I'm not going through with it."

"What the fuck," said Rat. "You've done most of the planning, you'd just fuck it all up for a woman?"

"If she writes back, she's a keeper and I won't feel like going through with it," he said.

"What about the rest of us?" Lenny said.

"I'm not stopping you going ahead. The plan still works without me and I'll stay out of the way when it's implemented."

"I don't know," said Angel. "You are the brains behind it. I don't know that I can go through with it if you're not with us any more."

"What the fuck kind of shit is that?" William said "It was Rat's suggestion in the first place. The same fucking shit will still be going on here, it will just be easier to handle day in, day out, if I have a woman in my life to care about. Anyway, it's not certain yet, she may not even write back."

William stood, followed by the others, to stack their trays and return to their section. They walked into the day room to spot a black and a Mexican inmate pushing and shoving each other, arguing about who was going to watch which TV show. During their dispute, Rat jumped onto the table and changed channel before either of them noticed.

Unfortunately for Rat, another black inmate had noticed and took offence. Rat leapt off the table, landing in front of the offended black inmate who said nothing to Rat, simply swinging around his fist, catching Rat a severe blow to his temple. Rat roared in pain, which alerted William, Lenny and Angel. They glanced around as Rat leapt on his attacker and several black inmates saw this action as a cue to fight. Within seconds there a full on brawl commenced between the black inmates and the white and Hispanics.

"Happy fucking Christmas," said William to no one in particular as he jumped into the fray.

As with all holidays and weekends, there was a massive shortage of staff, so no one came to break up the fighting up. The officer in the picket, seated in his chair, feet up on the desk, was watching and called for help. He'd been told that someone would come when available and, eventually, the newly promoted Lieutenant Wood entered. He shouted at the top of his voluminous voice.

"Stop fighting you fucking deranged animals. It's Christmas Day. Your choice, be racked up the rest of the day or stop fighting. I don't care."

"Wood, where are our Christmas movies we were promised?" said Angel. "No reason to stop fighting if we don't have movies to watch."

William and several others laughed and Angel's statement served to bring the fighting to an end, A truce was called, if only for one day.

45

There hadn't been any cell searches or beatings for a couple of weeks over the Christmas and New Year period, simply because few officers came to work during that time. They took their wages plus holiday pay and didn't turn in to work again until they had spent all of their money. There no risk to their jobs for TDCJ were so short of staff that they couldn't afford to fire people just for missing a few days work. Instead, the administration rewarded those who came into work by guaranteed over-time bonuses, extra days holidays, faster promotions and free good quality meals in the officers dining room, prepared and cooked by the very same inmates who would be fed sub-standard slop for their meals. Even incentives didn't work at some times of the year; no-one wanted to work Christmas or New Year/ Inmates spent most of the time over the holiday period racked up in their cells and it was already a time that inmates felt stressed and anxious as their thoughts turned to their family and children. The suicide rate amongst inmates shot up exponentially and it was little surprise to both officers and inmates when they discovered that more inmates had killed themselves.

Burton and his rogue cronies were no different and didn't turn in for work until after New Year. They were well rested and raring to return to exerting undue authority to those who could do little to retaliate.

"Jiggers on the floor," said a voice and the same message was passed around by different inmates, making sure that everyone in the section knew that the law was around. Everyone went silent as the Rogue Four, as they had been named, came in and peered around. They spotted Angel, Charlie, William, Teacher and his new cellie playing cards at the table.

"Doing a bit of gambling are you boys?" Burton asked and nobody replied.

"Hey old man, why the fuck are you playing cards with this bunch of losers?" said Flaherty. "Haven't seen you before. Fuck off before we think you're all friends."

"But we are all friends," said Charlie, forcing the officers to strain their ears to hear him as he continued, "You really don't want to fuck with me though."

"Oh and what makes you so fucking special Old Man?"

"I'm an expert at removing eyes," said Charlie, his eyes cold. He put his hand in his pocket and brought out two ping pong balls painted to represent eyes. He placed them on the table. "Here are two I removed earlier."

Flaherty and the other three officers took an involuntary step back. The eyes on the table had a macabre appearance and, coupled with Charlie's quiet, assured tone of voice, it sent a chill down their spines.

"They don't call him the Eyeball Killer for nothing," piped up a voice from the other side of the room."

The officers stared long and hard at Charlie, then, as one, turned away and decided to appear to ignore him.

"Who is this loser?" Burton said pointing at Angel's cellie, "I haven't seen you before. Just get here did you?Which is your house?"

FBI pointed without saying anything and Burton laughed.

"Well isn't that something? Boys we have some fresh blood at last and maybe he can give us a better fight then the rest of these pussy-ass girls."

The other three officers stared, reacting only with grins of anticipation on hearing Burton's words.

"Flaherty, Robinson, toss his cell. Everything. We don't want Angel thinking we've gone soft, and the new boy needs to learn how things are done around here."

Flaherty and Robinson cleared out the lockers onto the floor, made sure to stand on everything and break or damage as much as possible. They threw the mattresses up, pulled the sheets and blankets off and threw them on top of the toilet. Flaherty flushed repeatedly until the toilet was blocked and the water overflowed soaking the sheets and blankets, making them unusable. To finish their desecration, they ripped books apart, pulled photographs out of albums, tore up legal mail and then poured coffee over everything.

"Hey Angel," said Burton in an antagonising tone as Torres signalled to the picket officer to roll the doors.

"Rack up," he shouted. "Rack up now, you worthless motherfuckers. Fucking rack up now before we give all you losers a case for disobeying a direct order."

The inmates in the day-room and out on the runs moved towards their cells reluctantly for they knew what was coming and were all dreading it.

"Angel," repeated Burton. "You need to tell your mother to keep her mouth shut. She is going all over town talking shit about things she doesn't know or understand. Tell her to stop or she will be sorry."

"Oh yeah, what are you going to do, you corrupt piece of shit," said Angel, facing Burton.

FBI stood to walk to his cell but Robinson barred his way. "Sit yourself down boy and wait your turn."

At the same time Torres gave Angel a brutal punch to the kidneys and all hell let loose. Burton and Torres laid into Angel, who wasn't fully recovered from his pre-Christmas beatings. Robinson and Flaherty pounced on FBI who had just sat at the table as ordered so was in no position to defend himself.

The picket officer leant against the window watching the two beatings taking place. He watched Angel place few good retaliatory punches but, ultimately, he could not win against Burton and Torres. The officer smirked as he watched FBI, who was completely trounced. All FBI could do was to hunch low into the table and wait for the violence against him to stop.

"Not much of a fighter was he," said Flaherty. "Disappointing, never even turned round to try and fight. Fucking coward. Let's give him another chance. Hey Coward, stand up and fight. At least pretend to be a man."

FBI stood up slowly and backed away from the table. He turned around, head down and the four officers stared at him in disdain. Robinson was about to say something when, without warning, he received an unexpected punch in his gut. He doubled over for a moment then recovered slightly. With a growl he went for FBI at the same time as Flaherty and Burton did. Torres stayed back to hold Angel down and, in less than a minute, FBI was on the floor unable to move.

"We had better get these fucking losers to medical," said Torres grabbing hold of Angel's arm and pulling him to his feet. "Get up you fucking idiot."

Torres gave Angel a kick and Burton grabbed his other arm, shoving him roughly.

Robinson and Flaherty grabbed FBI's arms and half dragged half carried him along the hallways to the infirmary.

"You'd better tell that fucking mother of yours to shut the fuck up or she'll be getting more than a friendly cop visit to the house each day," said Burton.

"You're not the only one with influence. Anything happens to my mother you fucking piece of shit, you are the first one my people are coming to see," Angel said, "There is nothing in this world worse than a fucking corrupt piece of shit law enforcement officer. You're not even a fucking cop, you're an inmate babysitter."

"Keep running your mouth, see where that gets you, and more to the point your precious mother," Burton said as he stuck his foot in front of Angel's.

Both officers let go of his arms as Angel hit the concrete barely having chance to put an arm out to break his fall. He felt his wrist snap as the weight of his body landed on it.

"Fucking clumsy bastard. Why don't you watch what you're doing?" said Torres. "Fuck me, look at his arm, that has to hurt a bit, the bone has come through the skin."

FBI was listening as he watched what was happening in front of him. He kept mute, hoping his silence would prevent the same treatment befalling him.

Finally, they reached medical and Nurse Carling was on duty. She had spotted that the four officers were on duty, so had been expecting casualties. Despite the injuries she had seen on inmates previously from these officers, she was shocked when she inspected Angel's wrist.

"What happened to him?"

"No idea, the two of them were fighting. He was like this when we got to them, brought them straight over/" Burton said.

"Sit them down over there and get out of my infirmary."

The officers were surprised at her tone and Flaherty turned to argue with her, deciding against it when he saw the look on her face. The four of them gently placed Angel and FBI on to gurneys and left the room.

"Fuck, fuck, fuck," said Torres. "His arm was a real mess."

"We had better get our reports written. No one is going to dispute them if we all say the same thing." Burton said.

Nurse Carling had also produced her reports, complete with photos as back up. She called Sergeant Donovan and agreed to meet him and Captain Hauser after her shift was finished to give them the latest evidence for the ACLU investigation.

"How long will it be before they do something about it? They will kill someone else if they aren't stopped soon."

"Call me cynical, but TDCJ doesn't care about how many inmates are killed or injured. They only care that their wrong-doings aren't discovered. They will spend crazy amounts of money defending lawsuits, even when they are wrong. I've seen it over and over. They won't change unless they are forced to," said Captain Hauser.

"I am shocked at how many bad officers and staff there are working here," said Donovan.

"It's not just here, it's in every unit. There are plenty of officers and staff who care about what they are doing, try to be fair and do the job right, but there is a larger percentage who don't. So many are here for the wrong reason, they develop a power trip mentality, despise the inmates because they are inmates, so go out of their way to dehumanise them, making life harder for them. These are the problem officers; they have a de-stabilising influence, which leads to problems and ultimately to rioting. The biggest issue we have is poorly trained officers. You know yourself Donovan, your training was far from comprehensive."

"That is true, I've learnt more from Mad Dog on how to deal with situations than my training taught me."

"Mad Dog is a decent guy behind his very lengthy and volatile record. There isn't much he doesn't know about the system. He is still looking out for himself though, as all the inmates are. Never forget that."

"I've seen plenty of good, bad and worse officers over the years and those four officers are as bad as they come," Nurse Carling added.

"Yes they are," said Captain Hauser. "Things will move quickly now. Their inmate plant has been beaten up. He'll be called out to give a statement about what happened, at least that's what the inmates will think. When he sees the FBI and Texas Rangers, gives them his report, there will be a scramble for arrest warrants, then it's game over. I would say the next three to four days they'll be gone."

Just as Captain Hauser predicted, FBI was called to give his statement about the beating he received. Arrest warrants were issued and forty eight hours later Burton, Torres, Flaherty and Robinson were seen being handcuffed and escorted out of the prison. There were an additional sixteen officers arrested comprising seven corrections officers, three sergeants, three lieutenants, a captain, a major and the assistant warden.

The news spread like wildfire throughout the unit and the mood stayed upbeat for a couple of weeks until things returned to normal.

There were plenty of rumours about what happened to those who were arrested. For their parts in bringing the rogue officers to account, Hauser was promoted to Major and, as such, became a duty warden and Donovan was promoted to Lieutenant. The former assistant warden was transferred to a small minimum security unit. Lieutenant Wood and the other two lieutenants had convinced the investigators that they knew less than they actually did, so were rewarded with a mere transfer to a different unit. The corrections officers and sergeants were dismissed and the captain and major were both demoted one rank and transferred. Burton, Flaherty,

Torres and Robinson faced murder, harassment, falsifying official paperwork and actual bodily harm charges and Burton's brother was given an official reprimand for the harassment of Angel's mother. The police department refused to take it further, given the nature of the family business.

Angel's mother, being no shrinking violet, filed charges against both the police department, for harassment against herself, and TDCJ for both harassment and aggravated assault against her son.

47

"Are you coming to chow Mad Dog?" said Lenny.

"What are they feeding today?" William said.

"Chicken patties."

"No, I'll eat out of my locker."

"You don't want chicken?" Lenny said, his eyes wide with surprise.

"Not that fucking vitapro shit, no thank you. The mother-fuckers are doing their best to kill me by not giving me the medications I need. I'm not going to make it easy for them by eating that fucking poison they've starting feeding us," William said, his face bearing a grimace as he remembered eating it previously.

"It's good, I like it," said Lenny.

"You are fucking crazy, but then you always have been. Always got to try something when you don't know what's in it. It's the same with fucking dope, the stronger and more dangerous the better. You're a fucking idiot."

Meat substitute had been fed to them recently and William had tried it and spat it out. It tasted bad, but also had an alarming side effect in those who ate it regularly. As most of the inmates were indigent, having little outside support to permit them the luxury of buying food from commissary, they had to eat the sub-standard slop at every meal. Shortly after introducing the meat substitute, these inmates developed angry rashes and sores on their bodies. The infirmary was inundated with visits complaining about the unexplained skin condition. For a while the medical staff were puzzled, unsure what was causing the malaise, doling out tubes of cream to help clear up the affliction, to no avail.

"What the fuck have you done to your arm?" William said as he watched Lenny scratch furiously at an angry red spot on it.

"Fucked if I know, but I've got rashes all over my body. One of them on my leg is really bad, it keeps weeping. The cream they gave me in medical doesn't make any difference."

"I don't want to fucking see it," said William as Lenny pulled his trouser leg up. "Nor do I want to catch it if it's contagious."

"I think it must be," said Lenny. "I've seen loads of guys scratching, they've rashes too."

"Well fucking stay away from me until you've got rid of it. The last thing I need is another health issue, I have enough as it is."

Lenny laughed as he headed off to the chow hall.

The desk officer shouted over to William as she put the phone down and told him that Lieutenant Donovan had called him out, to go and see him. William made his way to their usual meeting spot and Donovan was scratching his hand as William walked through the door.

"Not you too, what the fuck is going on. Everyone is scratching.

"That's what I wanted to talk to you about," Donovan said as he handed over eight baggies of weed. William tucked them away without giving them more than a cursory glance.

"I heard that the Director of TDCJ had become a spokesman for the company who supplies this new meat substitute. I went to talk it over with Major Hauser and he told me the same thing, he'd checked to see if it was true. Well, it seems that the Director has some lucrative sideline deal going on."

"Wouldn't that be a conflict of interest?"

"That's what Major Hauser and I thought, so we started doing some research into this Vitapro stuff." Donovan said and stopped talking a moment whilst he looked at his very sore rash in disgust, unable to resist scratching it again, wincing as he did .

"So what did you find out?" William said, his interest piqued.

Donovan's face looked grim as he explained to William that both Vitapro beef and Vitapro chicken were foodstuffs fed to pigs. Water would be added to the dried foodstuff to bulk it up and make it go further. All the pigs being fed it had developed open sores.

William's face Developed a stern appearance as he said, "So the fucking director of TDCJ has contracted to buy pigswill to feed to inmates and the feed company pay him a fortune to do it."

"Absolutely," said Donovan. "Worse, it's illegal to feed it to humans."

"Come on now Donovan, you know inmates aren't considered humans, only animals to be fed pigswill for some crooked mother-fucker to make a fortune," William said, now cross.

Donovan had a look of distress on his face as he said, "How can they do it? It is so wrong."

"You are too good for this job Donovan," said William, laughing, "You'd better go to medical and get that rash looked at. That has to be what is causing everyone to develop sores."

"Don't you have any?"

"I'm not stupid enough to eat that slop. Did you talk to the Vampire about it?"

"Not yet, I'll go and talk to her now. Come with me. You can have her check you over for any signs."

Nurse Carling and the other nurses on duty were run off their feet, prescribing a generic cream to the huge numbers of inmates turning up to have their skin conditions treated. She looked up when William and Lieutenant Donovan came in.

"I haven't time for your hundreds of health problems right now, Mad Dog," she said, tapping away on the computer keyboard, entering notes about inmates treatment into their medical files.

"Donovan has come to talk to you about what's going on."

She looked at Donovan's face and groaned as she said, "Not another scandal you're dragging me into?"

"Just a little scandal," said William.

"Mad Dog, it's serious," said Donovan.

William feigned seriousness as he said, "You're damned right it's serious. It's like the time a maintenance manager back in the nineties during a spurt of prison building stole air-conditioning units and fully grown pigs to sell for himself. Or the time a

Mexican sergeant was running a drug and prostitution ring. Or the time someone got a gun in the unit and got so scared he asked me to get rid of it. Someone snitched after I disposed of it and they sent every mother-fucker and their dogs in to find it."

Donovan and Nurse Carling looked equally aghast at what William had told them.

"Don't stand there like a pair of demented lunatics on the run from the asylum," William said.

"We'd better go in my office," said Nurse Carling.

The other nurses stared at her, annoyed that she was leaving them to do all of the work. The fact that Nurse Carling had a trying time each day, just to cajole them to do the basic aspects of their jobs, didn't factor in their thoughts. The nurses tried to do as little as possible and hated it when their hospital employer sent them to work shifts at the prison. The leering men who wanted to chat them up and more disgusted them and they had all, at some time, been subjected to inmates jacking off whilst they talked to them.

One of the nurses had tried to flirt with William but he had rejected her by laughing and she had felt humiliated. A woman scorned, she now hated him and did everything to prevent him from receiving the medical care he needed. She would be happy for him to die, especially when she saw William smirking at them as he entered the office and closed the door.

"So what's going on now?" said Nurse Carling.

Lieutenant Donovan told her about the meat substitute, side effects and the role of the TDCJ Director.

Nurse Carling looked thoughtful for a minute, before saying, "I heard the warden and the assistant warden talking about it. They said that they wouldn't mind a slice of the pie. Now I understand what they were talking about."

"Is that what's causing the rashes and sores on everyone?" Donovan said.

"I would say so. Can't be certain until we do tests, but it looks that way. I suspected something wasn't right. It's abnormal to have so many cases, with the same distinctive symptoms. I couldn't say for certain what had caused it so couldn't prescribe anything specific to treat the condition."

"Can you do what you did before and write your own separate files and hand them to the Health Department?" said William.

"Yes I will, but I think we need to the Health Department involved immediately.

"How about we do it like last time? You give your files to me and Major Hauser and we can take them to the Health Department. We get them involved by showing them the files, in person."

"Works for me. I'll work on them now, and we can meet the same place as last time to hand them over."

"Come on Mad Dog, I'll walk you back to make sure you get back to your house intact," Donovan said giving him a knowing look. The last thing either of them wanted was for William to be stripped out and the eight baggies discovered.

Nurse Carling looked at William wistfully as he left.

Oh well, I'm far too busy anyway. Next time, she thought to herself.

A few days later, gossip and stories flew around the unit yet again when the health department turned up to take skin samples from affected inmates and the pigs being reared on the farm. They also took away samples of the swill being fed to the pigs, and the slop being fed to the inmates. It took months to run all of the tests conclusively and, all the while, the inmates continued to be fed the illegal foodstuff. The FBI had been called in to investigate the feeding of animal products to inmates and had questioned why the inmates weren't being fed with food produced from the unit's massive farm, which included pigs, beef, dairy and dozens of different crops being grown. TDCJ had no answer. T They were using free inmate labour to sell their produce for top market value and could feed the inmates for less on the food supplements or buying out of date food.

The circumstances of the TDCJ Director's involvement as a paid spokesperson for the feed company were investigated and they found that he was being paid tens of thousands a month to promote the product for the feed company. The warden and assistant warden were questioned about what they knew and Nurse Carling told the investigators of the conversation she'd overheard between the two of them. Ultimately the Director was arrested. He had signed a lucrative contract with the feed company to supply the entirety of TDCJ units and other prisons and jails, especially those interested in cutting the cost of feeding their incarcerated populations.

He faced federal charges bribery, money laundering and conspiracy and served eighteen months in a federal prison, albeit a soft one.

48

When William arrived back on his section he saw Angel talking to a new guy who had recently been transferred. He fetched himself a drink of cold water and sat down at the table with them.

"Mad Dog, this is Gideon." Angel said as William held out his hand to shake that of the newcomer, "He's my new cellie, got here a few days ago."

"I see you're Ace Deuce," said William glancing at his affiliation tattoos, using the alternative term for the Aryan Brotherhood.

"Sergeant at Arms for West Texas," Gideon said, as he started to chuckle, "Got three life sentences stacked for killing three worthless Bloods who tried to rob one of our repair shops. I couldn't convince the jury that I was doing the world a favour getting rid of the mother-fuckers."

Gideon went onto explain that he had done five years in segregation for stabbing a female corrections officer at his previous unit because she had taken his typewriter away. She'd survived, unfortunate in Gideon's opinion as he'd aimed to kill her. Five years in seg had reinforced his conviction that he needed to kill an officer to be moved onto Death Row so that the administration would have to end his life. He was never leaving prison, having to serve almost three hundred years, but he was not of a mind to kill himself. In his mind, Death Row was the only option left.

William and Angel nodded, recognising his plight.

"Can you believe those mother-fuckers came into my shop and tried to steal some of our bikes. A fucking Blood on our Harley's, they'd look stupid, man. It's bad enough the mother-fuckers don't talk properly. refusing to say any word beginning with C," he said, disgust clear from his voice and countenance.

"That is so fucked up," said William, chortling, "Bloods won't say words with C, or they change the C to a different letter and the fucking Crips do the same with the letter B. They should just kill each other and be done with it."

"Worthless bitch-ass mother-fuckers, all of them," said Angel.

They continued their mocking of the two black gangs, themselves bitter rivals, by mocking the way they talked.

"Are you cowards too scared to take a heating," said Gideon.

"Pan I get a packet of tortilla thips and a foke," said William, laughing deeply.

"A pint of ice-fream would be good too, thocolate frownie flavour," said Angel.

The three laughed hysterically at the absurdity of the gang rules; the reality was different; If a Crip used the letter B, and a Blood used the letter C, they could be killed by one of their own. Life was cheap.

It spurred William, Angel and Gideon on, when members of the gangs in question took offence and threatened to beat them. The three laughed, inviting them to bring their A game. On that occasion their offer to fight was declined due to lack of numbers but William said nothing, instead he pulled his shirt up to expose a crude tattoo on the side of his ribcage. It was a picture of a penis with the words 'SUCK MY' etched above it. The black gangsters were furious and threatened retaliation.

"Fring it on you fucking coward-ass losers," said Gideon, guaranteeing that a fight would ensue in the near future.

Officer Arturo came into the section and he was mad. He'd had an argument with his girlfriend that morning and she'd waved him a final goodbye. He was on a mission and didn't notice the inmate he bumped into.

"Watch what you're fucking doing, you fucking loser," he said at the white guy on whose heels he had trodden. Charlie turned, pulling his hand out of his pocket and held his two ping-pong eyes up in front of his real ones and leaned into Arturo.

"Talk to the eyes, because I don't give a fuck bitch," he said.

Arturo recoiled in horror at the lifelike eyes. Realising who he'd walked into, Arturo stepped away from the crazy guy with an eye fetish. *Absolute sickos some of these inmates*, he thought to himself. Now he was really ready to take out his bad mood on some inmates and one inmate in particular.

"You," he said, addressing Teacher. "Where are all your buddy boys. I don't see any of them."

He didn't wait for an answer but strode over to Angel and Gideon's cell and Gideon looked up from what he was doing. He had spent the morning pulling out the threads from his boxer shorts and making a fine rope on which he could then use to hang his washing, or his towel for privacy when he wished to use the toilet or perform other personal activities.

"What the fuck do you want bitch?"

"Where is your loser cellie?" Arturo said, choosing to ignore Gideon's hostile tone; there would be an opportunity to deal with his disrespect later.

"I'm here Bitch," said Angel from behind, wearing only his shorts and shower slides, having stepped from the shower. He held his wet towel in his hands, twisting it end to end giving the impression that it was a thick rope. Anything in prison could be used as a weapon with some imagination. Angel kept twisting it, in case he needed to use the towel for other than it's intended purpose.

"Nice to see you Angel, how are you?" he said as he spun around, a menacingly smooth tone to his voice.

Addressing Gideon briefly, he told him to leave the cell and Gideon stood, picking up a few objects to take into the day room with him as soon as the door rolled open. Arturo stepped into the cell and started tossing Angel and Gideon's property around. Arturo pulled items out of the inmate's lockers and swilled Gideon's cup of coffee that was on top of his locker A bottle of bleach that Angel had bought at commissary the previous day was opened and poured over the mess on the floor. Arturo picked up something from under Angel's mattress, studying the plastic bag full of a white powder. He stepped back out of the cell and stared at Angel, a grin on his face.

"Well look what I just found under your mattress Angel." Arturo said as he opened the bag and dipped in his finger tip. He licked his finger to taste the substance. "Looks like I've caught you trading in Heroin, naughty, naughty boy."

"You fucking planted that, you fucking low life shit-head," Angel said.

"Why would I do that, when you leave it lying around for me to find so easily?"

"I've never touched that shit in my life and everyone knows it, "Angel said, shouting in Arturo's face.

"Well there it was for everyone to see," Arturo said, "Only one place for you to go now. I'll make sure you get the dirtiest, darkest, dampest cell and that's more than a mother-fucker like you deserves," he said as spittle hit Angel's face as Arturo's tone changed to venomous.

Gideon had been standing behind the officer during the exchange and had been studying his newly made rope, testing it's strength by yanking the ends apart, as he listened intently to the dialogue as it unfolded. He didn't like the way this mother-fucker was talking to his cellie and new friend. Angel and Gideon had hit it off and that inspired loyalty. It had taken him by surprise that he had such a rapport with a non-white person, for it hadn't happened before. Gideon wasn't going to see his friend set up but, as importantly, he saw a way to achieve his own goal. Whilst Arturo was in full flow, verbally abusing Angel, Gideon stepped towards him and, quick as a flash, brought his rope around his neck and pulled tightly so that the rope was cutting into Arturo's Adam's Apple. Gideon used Arturo's weight and his struggling to to his advantage and the cord dug deeper into the officer's neck. Arturo had dropped the bag of white powder when his hands shot up to his neck and Angel bent down to retrieve it, stepping away to give the packet to Carlos One to hold. Gideon knew that he was achieving his aim when he felt Arturo's windpipe crush so he tightened the cord more. Arturo's struggles grew less as he struggled for breath until his knees buckled and Gideon followed him to the floor, keeping up the pressure. Gideon kept a tight hold of his home-made ligature for a good minute after Arturo had stopped struggling. Gideon wanted to be certain that there wasn't a breath left in Arturo. Eventually he released the pressure and pulled the rope from around the officer's neck.

During the altercation between Arturo and Angel, a small crowd of guys had formed around them in the day room. They watched as events unfolded and, when they realised an officer was dead, they slunk away, not wanting to be implicated in the murder. They couldn't enter their cells, which weren't open, so they went and sat at the tables furthest away from Angel's cell and busied themselves playing cards, dominoes or watching television, anything to give the appearance that they had no part in the incident when rank turned up to deal with it. They need not have been concerned, for Gideon was happy to confess to the murder of the worthless corrupt and lying officer.

The picket officer had gone to watch over another section and had fallen asleep so had no idea what had transpired and the desk officer had visited the bathroom as Officer Arturo came in. She returned a few minutes later and noticed the strange atmosphere in the room. She scanned the area and her eyes came to rest on Gideon who was seated on a table, feet on a stool with a contented smile on his face. She was puzzled until she looked around him and saw the officer lying on the floor, his tongue protruding in an unnatural way. Then, the sixty year old bowling ball on legs gave a piercing scream startling those inmates who were trying to pretend that they knew nothing. She snatched the two way radio from her belt and screamed into it *for back up immediately*, officer down. There was static during the response, making it indecipherable to anyone except the officer who had the receiver next to her ear.

"Keep back, keep back," she screamed in a high shrill tone which didn't match her appearance.

One of the black inmates pretending to play cards said in response, "What are you talking about Bitch? No one is doing anything."

It was five minutes before an officer and three rank came running into the section: Officer Stead, Sergeant Huntley, who had received promotion for helping to save William's life, Lieutenant Shandy, who had replaced Hardy and a captain. Lieutenant Shandy took charge as Officer Stead and Sergeant Huntley checked Arturo over.

"What the fuck did you do mother-fucker?" Shandy said, addressing Gideon. "Where's that fucking Mad Dog? He has to have something to do with it, always wrapped up in every type of shit that's going on."

Hardy and Shandy were friends, having trained and risen through the ranks together and Shandy was aware of Hardy's hatred for William.

"He's in the law library," said Angel.

"That doesn't mean he doesn't have anything to do with this. Whoever had a part in the killing of my officer, I will personally make sure they go to Death Row."

"Well it wasn't fucking Mad Dog," said Angel, "You haven't been here long, do you even know who he fucking is?"

"I know all about that waste of space mother-fucker," Shandy said.

Gideon stood up from the table. "I killed the corrupt worthless mother-fucker, me and only me. I'll happily kill another if it gets me sent to Death Row and you mother-fuckers have to murder me," he said.

Lieutenant Shandy voice betrayed his outrage as he said, "You fucking piece of shit. He was one of my best officers and you'll pay big time for this."

Everyone in the room burst into cynical laughter, loudly voicing contempt at Shandy's declaration.

"If that worthless bitch was one of your finest, it explains why all the other useless fucking trash-ass bitches are so bad," said Gideon, "You had better check that I killed him. I don't want the mother-fucker to still be breathing."

"You fucking piece of shit," said Shandy, shouting into Gideon's face, "I'll…" but the rest of his sentence remained unsaid.

"Lieutenant Shandy," said Captain Kuznets, her voice booming "Control yourself. Conduct yourself in a professional manner."

Considered a decent officer by the inmates, she had been transferred to the unit after the officer beating inmates scandal. Nicknamed Captain Russia because she had a mild but noticeable Russian accent, she was determined to clean up the unit and was intolerant of unprofessional or retaliatory behaviour towards inmates. Neither would she tolerate behaviour that demeaned her as a woman. She had worked hard to become Captain and wouldn't permit disrespect towards her person. Kuznets was a 'strictly by the book' officer, so inmates knew exactly where they stood with her. Lieutenant Shandy and his cronies did not like her, exactly for those reasons. She had been holding them to account far too often for their liking, and Shandy was at risk of a demotion again, which was not in his long term game plan. He had been demoted from Captain at his previous unit, hence the transfer.

"Officer Bowles, call over to medical to bring a gurney," Kuznets said.

The inmates sniggered at hearing Bowles name, apt considering her bowling ball shape. Captain Kuznets gave them a fierce glare which silenced them As she said, "Lieutenant Shandy, you will accompany Officer Arturo to the infirmary. Sergeant Huntley and Officer Stead, please take Gideon to lock up. Angel pack up Gideon's property for him."

Lieutenant Shandy glared at both Captain Kuznets and Officer Stead. Despite being of higher rank, Shandy hated Stead for attempting to keep him in check when Stead considered that Shandy was out of control. Stead had worked on two previous units with Shandy and he had been the same temperament there. As Gideon was escorted away by Officer Stead, he turned to Angel and winked.

"What the fuck happened." said William as he returned a short while later. I saw Huntley and Stead taking Gideon to jail."

"Arturo won't be a problem any more," Angel said, "Gideon took care of him."

"He's a good mother-fucker. Shame Gideon won't be around any more."

49

William was lying on his bunk listening to his radio when he saw the officer push an envelope under his door. Mail was a huge deal in prison and he rarely received any. He jumped up and picked the envelope off the floor; the package was well stuffed and the handwriting unfamiliar. There were no sender details in the top left corner. William turned the envelope over in his hands and saw that the return address was written on the back. Unusual, William had never seen it done like that before.

Ireland! She'd written back.

He tore open the envelope and took out a six page letter, reading the entire letter standing on the spot, too eager to discover the content to make himself comfortable. By the time he'd finished reading it his eyes were shining and felt an excitement and anticipation that he hadn't experienced before. He looked at the name on the envelope, then gave it a kiss; she had written back, he couldn't believe it, had butterflies in his stomach and felt a warm tingle.

William made himself as comfortable as was possible on his steel bunk with its cardboard thin mattress. With a grin spreading across his face, William re-read the most amazing letter he had ever received. At that moment he knew, for him at least, the plan to end his life and long term stay in prison was over.

50

William had been writing to Helen for almost a year. They were writing three letters a week to each other. A short letter of under twelve pages, a medium length letter of twenty pages and a long letter of over twenty pages. Anything under eight pages they considered a note. William didn't have a job as he had medical restrictions which severely limited what he was allowed to do. He was happy with this; formerly it gave him plenty of time to do as he pleased, see who he wanted and break as many rules as he could get away with. It had always been his mission to flow against the current, get one over on the system. Now, much of that time was spent writing letters to the love of his life.

Others would see him scribe, page after page. His writing hand would have trouble keeping up with his voluminous thoughts. He would be asked about his letters constantly: *what was there to talk about? Nothing ever happens here.* Inmates told of how letters to their loved ones would be only a few lines and William scoffed, telling them that he wouldn't waste a stamp to send a couple lines. Even his close friends couldn't understand how he managed to write so much each week.

"What the fuck do you write about?" Lenny said, "The same things in every letter?"

"Are you fucking crazy," William said "Why would I waste postage on writing the same shit? We talk about anything and everything in our letters. The letters she sends me are amazing."

He read out a short section out from the letter he was currently answering. She described some of the places she would visit on her tours around Europe, the places, what people in her groups would say or do and the problems that would occur. These letters were accompanied by photographs and postcards corresponding to Helen's travels. William had guys constantly asking to see his photos. To the inmates, they were unique as most of the guys had only photos of children and family or hustle photos of scantily clad women. These photos could be rented for a time or bought from the inmate who owned them. None of the inmates had seen the types of photographs that William received: stunning landscapes, fairytale castles, cliffs, lakes and magnificent gardens. The colours were a source of amazement too as they were used to seeing the barren Texan landscape caused by the scorching sun. William adored his photographs and was fiercely protective of them, particular about to whom he showed them. Officers would come and ask to see the pictures and there would always be wishes to travel to these places, one day. As was the way, many inmates were jealous of William; he had something that they didn't, and others would ask if Helen could find them someone to write to. William had asked her for a few of his friends and she'd told him that she would see what she could do but that it wouldn't be easy as most people didn't want to be involved with an inmate. After William had asked a few times, Helen lost her patience with him, telling him that she wasn't running an inmate dating service. William desisted and passed this message on to his associates.

As time went on and William became more invested in his friendship and burgeoning relationship with his new love, there was increasing jealousy from other inmates, not helped by the fact that William bragged, to any one who would listen, about how wonderful Helen was. He waxed lyrical about the places she visited, things she did, and the stories she told him. He couldn't last five minutes without making her the topic of conversation. Guys he had never spoken to would talk, out of earshot, about him, their fingers pointing his way. Sometimes, not quite out of earshot so that he would hear them, they'd utter *'Who does he think he is. Look at him. How could he get any woman? I could take her from him. Can we get her address and write to her.'* William would laugh and tell them that they wouldn't have a chance with his girl; she had more taste than to be interested in losers like them. That riled them, making several of the inmates determined to ruin things for William. He was streetwise, knowing that haters always tried to wreck the relationships of inmates who had someone on the outside and it didn't have to be a wife or girlfriend, often it was family members or friends. Anyone who showed consistent support for an inmate would become a target for the haters. William, and every other inmate who valued their loved ones, went to great lengths to ensure that contact information couldn't be obtained. In William's case, as soon as he received a letter, he removed the return address from the envelope and tore it into tiny pieces and flushed the pieces down the toilet in his cell. It was never guaranteed that an address would remain secret. Mail would often be delivered to the wrong inmate, usually because they had been moved to a different cell or building, sometimes by accident and, on occasion, on purpose. Rarely did the correct inmate then receive his mail as letters were a precious commodity in prison. To be gifted with a letter, even by mistake, was a blessing, especially for those with sinister motives. At the least, it caused upset and paranoia for the inmate for which the mail was intended and, at best, the letter would provide an inmate with information that could be used against the intended recipient as blackmail and extortion were commonplace behind bars, just another way of conducting trade for both survival and comfort. William didn't worry too much about others writing to Helen as he knew that they wouldn't spend money on the three stamps minimum it cost to send a letter overseas. Still, he left nothing that he had any control over to chance.

William came bursting out of his cell as soon as the lazy officer decided to run an in and out. He had been talking to Rat and Teacher through his door but they had now gone to work. He headed straight over to Lenny, Angel and Carlos One at their table. He was bubbling over with excitement and couldn't wait to tell everyone.

"She's coming to see me," he said, his voice raised.

"Who?" said the three guys in unison, taken aback at his outburst.

"Who the fuck do you think, fucking idiots. Helen has booked a flight and will be coming to see me."

"What the fuck would she want to come and see you for?" Lenny said.

"She's coming all the way from Europe?" Carlos One said.

"She must be crazy," mused Angel. "Does she know you are a crazy mother-fucker?"

"Of course, she knows everything about me," said William, unable to keep a grin off his face.

"What do you mean by everything?" Lenny said, a hint of concern in his voice.

"Everything. I told her everything I've done. I said if she wrote back, there wouldn't be any secrets, so I've told her everything."

"Why would you tell her everything if you don't need to? It's not like she'd know, if you didn't say anything," Angel said.

"You lot are idiots. With all these haters, do you think I want someone else telling her about things I've done and putting their own twist on it. No fucking way. I would rather she hear it from me."

"No way would I be telling anyone everything I've done," said Lenny.

"You've no need to, I've told her a lot of what you've done," said William.

"What the fuck Mad Dog, why did you do that?"

"Chill out Lenny, only the stuff we did together," William said.

"But what if she tells the law, she could get us in a lot of trouble," Lenny said.

"Don't be such a drama queen Lenny. The statute of limitations is long over on everything we did together. As for me, if she decides to end things with me then I won't be hanging around anyway."

"Ok," said Lenny.

"Anyway the most important thing is that she's coming to see me," William said as he danced around the table ruffling each of his friend's hair in turn. He was excited and nothing could spoil his mood.

51

William was woken up by the sound of a fight outside his door. The cursing and profanity, along with the two bodies hitting his door causing it to rattle loudly on it's runners roused him out of a dead sleep.

"What the fuck?"

He jumped up from his bunk, narrowly missing smacking his head on the steel bunk above him. He looked through the toughened glass in his door, albeit hazily because of the scratches and scuffs which were evident on all of the doors that hadn't yet had the glass kicked out of them. He saw Carlos Two beating the black who had caused Spider's death in the riot. He was punching the same spot on the guy's temple repeatedly. Carlos Two was too preoccupied to hear William's shouts to move away from his door. Lieutenant Shandy came into the day room looking for two of his workers who hadn't turned into work in the laundry. He spotted the fight, took note of William shouting through his door, and called for back-up on his radio. The rover officer came at a run from the pod next door and they strode over to the fighting inmates. Lieutenant Shandy pulled out his canister of pepper spray and aimed it straight in the faces of the two fighters. It took a few moments for the burning effects of the spray to register but, when it did, both inmates dropped to the floor, the black inmate because he was beaten half to death. Carlos Two dropped onto his hands and knees to cough and splutter the spray out of his mouth and was wiping his eyes when his arms were yanked behind his back, handcuffs attached and a boot on his back pushed him over to lie on the floor. The rover officer tried to handcuff the black inmate but he was unresponsive on the floor, other than to groan in agony.

Lieutenant Shandy shouted to the desk officer to call for a nurse and a wheelchair. He also signalled to the picket officer to open William's cell door.

"Turn round and hands behind your back, mother-fucker," he shouted at William.

"What the fuck for?"

"You're going to lock-up with these two idiots."

"Again, what the fuck for?"

"I'm writing you up for incitement to riot."

"Are you fucking crazy, bitch?" William said, "Those mother-fuckers woke me out of a dead sleep banging my door."

"Not what it looked like from where I was standing," Shandy said his face decorated with a smirk.

"Fucking worthless lying-ass bitch. Anyone, including that worthless picket officer, can tell you I was asleep. He can see straight into my cell."

"Tell it to someone who cares. You are going to jail."

William chose to ignore Shandy's order to turn round and be cuffed. Instead, he dressed himself and started packing his things up. When he finished, he plonked back down onto his bunk, waiting to be escorted to lock-up. He knew how the system worked and that Shandy would fabricate a bad enough case to give him seg time.

"Sorry Mad Dog," said Carlos Two as they waited together in the small cage to be processed for confinement into twelve building which housed segregation and closed custody. Closed custody was not considered to be segregation, although the distinction was minor; the same conditions applied, twenty three hours a day locked up, restrictions for commissary and recreation. The only difference was there were two in the cell instead of the inmate being alone.

"Don't worry about it, it's no big deal. What the fuck was the fight about?"

"That piece of shit was on his own at the table. He was the one who finished Spider off, so I jumped him. Didn't get chance to finish him off though."

"He didn't look like he'd be ok any time soon. You trounced him good and proper, hitting him in the same spot over and over. Who knows what that has done to the bitch. He deserved it anyway. I don't think we need to lose any sleep over him."

William and Carlos Two shared a cell in closed custody until they went to their UCC hearings. Lieutenant Shandy had made up lies on his report, writing that William had encouraged the fight. He fabricated conversations that William was supposed to have had about it but, naturally, the allegations were not investigated. The prisoners that William was supposed to have had conversations with were not questioned, and William was found guilty. The officers holding court weren't known to William and his protestations were ignored, considered the classic lies of an inmate. He was given two years in closed custody and Carlos Two was given one.

"We may as well start as we mean to go on Carlos," William said when he returned to the cell from his hearing, "We are in the five star hotel so let's make those mother-fuckers work for us."

"Works for me," Carlos said , "Angel and the guys have sent us some goodies over. How about we have ourselves a good dinner. Blaine sent a kite and some soups over too."

52

It was the day of William's first visit. He was excited, anxious and nervous, all at the same time. The guys were keeping out of his way; they had been hearing for two weeks about Helen's impending visit. Although they were happy for William - particularly as he never had visits, other than a rare one from his mother, it was wearing on their nerves hearing about it continually, particularly how wonderful and perfect Helen was. It was a reminder to the guys who didn't have anyone or didn't receive visits of what they were missing.

William hadn't slept well for two days and had dark circles under his eyes. He was worried that something would happen and Helen wouldn't make it, that she'd changed her mind or something happened to the plane. He hadn't slept at all for the duration of her travels, about twenty hours. William knew that she'd arrived the previous day and, apart from hiring a car and finding her hotel, the only thing left was to find a bank and change twenty dollars into quarters for the vending machine in the visitation room.

He was mad with himself for being in closed custody as she had to travel from the other side of the world to visit him from behind glass, speaking through a telephone handset. He felt guilty about it.

What if she was so freaked out she wouldn't visit again? What if she didn't like him when she saw him? The way he looked. The way he spoke. The tattoos over his head, now obvious courtesy of having a shaved head. What if she was turned off by the four missing bottom front teeth which had been knocked out by someone's lucky punch?

He could feel his elevated blood pressure.

He arose early to be ready when she arrived. Helen had told him in her last letter that she would be at the prison after lunch. He had an extended shower, spending an hour washing and shaving off every hair on his body. He had got a new set of clothes from the necessity supplies department next to the laundry. He wanted to look as good as he could under the circumstances. He couldn't understand guys who waited to be called for a visit before heading for the shower and cleaning themselves up. William considered it to be disrespectful to those who went to the effort of visiting and it wasn't always straightforward. The units were usually located 'in the middle of nowhere'. Public transport was non-existent and visitors were subjected to pat-down searches and disdain from officers. Despite TDCJ's official policy of encouraging family and friend visitation, making a visit was neither easy nor pleasant.

For Helen, there was an added element of uncertainty as she had to call several days in advance to request a special visit. As she was coming from a great distance, she could request a visit of four hours on both Saturday and Sunday and an inmate could have one of these visits a month, a regular visit being two hours on either Saturday or Sunday, but not both. She had to call on the Friday before the visit to check it was approved, and would be travelling then; by Wednesday or Thursday she'd have to check and hope they had already approved it.

Given the efforts and hoops Helen that had to jump through to visit him, he was damned sure he wasn't going to keep her waiting.

"Mad Dog, visit. Hurry up," shouted Sergeant Huntley when she came to fetch him. The officers had also been subjected to his excitement over his impending visit. They were curious and surprised that someone from the other side of the world would visit an inmate in prison. The guys all appeared to give him encouragement.

"Wish me luck," William said to them as he looked at them each in turn. "This is it."

"Enjoy your visit Mad Dog."

"Don't keep her waiting Mad Dog."

"Don't go playing the fool mother-fucker."

"Don't say anything stupid like you usually do Mad Dog."

"Don't scare her off Mad Dog."

William was beyond 'ready to go'. His stomach was churned one minute and dancing with butterflies the next.

"Mad Dog come on, what the fuck are you waiting for?" shouted Huntley.

Coming from closed custody he had to be escorted whilst handcuffed.

"Sorry about the cuffs Mad Dog. I hope it won't freak her out to see them."

"Me too, Huntley, but I don't think it will."

The high security building where segregation and closed custody were housed, had its own visitation room. It was long and narrow with a row of twelve cubicles, each being a separate visiting booth. On the visitors side, the cubbyholes were divided by a vertical partition wall, housing a telephone handset on each side, enough for two visitors who would sit on a narrow wooden bench fixed to the dirty grey concrete floor. On the wall behind the visitor were three vending machines, two filled with snacks and sandwiches, the third with a collection of soft drinks. Next to the vending machines was a table where two officers supervised the visits. On the table was a stack of compartmentalised food trays. When the visitor bought food, the officer would empty the contents from the packaging onto the tray and take it around to the inmate.

William and Sergeant Huntley walked down the long corridor. Travelling in the opposite direction was another escorted inmate, hands cuffed behind his back. As they drew nearer to each other William recognised the man and his senses were heightened.

"How are the finances, Big Man?" William said, provocatively.

"Fuck you motherfucker. You'll pay for what you did."

William smirked. As the two drew alongside each other with their escorts, William noticed a movement and instinctively sidestepped out of Mighty Mouth's reach.

Just in time.

Mighty Mouth had slipped one hand from his handcuffs and, in a fluid movement, removed a razor he had hidden against the gum of his mouth and lashed out. Unfortunately for Huntley, she became the unintended target. She screamed as the blade sliced open her shoulder blade and the escort officer jumped on top of Mighty Mouth in an attempt to stop him. Huntley's screams brought Major Hauser and Officer Stead running from the Warden's office. It took all three of them to restrain Mighty Mouth.

After Mighty Mouth had been led away, Officer Stead turned to William. "For fuck's sake Mad Dog, can't we have one day in which you're not involved in some sort of shit."

Lightning Source UK Ltd.
Milton Keynes UK
UKHW010634040321
379777UK00001B/207